SPEAKER
FOR THE
POWERLESS

Conversations We'd Have if
Our Leaders Could Hear Us

TODD LEDERMAN

Elk Meadow Press
Evergreen, Colorado, USA

Photo Credits:
Cover Photo montage — Bill Maher photo courtesy of Angela George;[1][2] Photos created for the United States Senate — Elizabeth Warren created by Gage Skidmore, John McCain created by Adam Barker, Bernie Sanders, and Marco Rubio — are in the public domain; "Make America Think Again" courtesy of Mark Dixon;[1][4] Women's March on Washington courtesy of Mobilus in Mobili.[1][5]
Back Cover — Occupy Wall St. protest courtesy of David Shankbone;[2] Tea Party protest courtesy of Sage Ross;[6] Boston Tea Party is a faithful reproduction of an 1846 lithograph now in the public domain in the United States because it was published before January 1, 1923.
Radical American Terrorists montage — Timothy McVeigh, Scott Roeder, Paul Jennings Hill, Eric Rudolph, Clayton Lee Waagner, Colonel John Chivington, Philip Klingensmith, Isaac C. Haight, Maj. John H. Higbee, Wade Michael Page, Maj. John D. Lee, and Dylann Roof — photos all in public domain.
May 3, 1963 Birmingham firefighters blasting protesters — photo in public domain.
Donkey photo courtesy of Pixabay.com; Elephant photo courtesy of Yathin S. Krishnappa;[1][3]

Art Credits:
Argument Before the Supreme Court, Half Robot — Todd Lederman self portrait (Copyright © 2017 by Todd Lederman) with half robot effect courtesy of pho.to from http://funny.pho.to/half-robot-face-mask/

1 Licensed under Creative Commons (https://en.wikipedia.org/wiki/Creative_Commons)
2 Licensed under Attribution 3.0 Unported (https://creativecommons.org/licenses/by/3.0/deed.en)
3 Licensed under Attribution-Share Alike 3.0 Unported (https://creativecommons.org/licenses/by-sa/3.0/deed.en)
4 Licensed under Attribution 2.0 Generic (https://creativecommons.org/licenses/by/2.0/deed.en)
5 Licensed under Attribution-Share Alike (https://creativecommons.org/licenses/by-sa/2.0/deed.en)
6 Licensed under GNU Free Documentation License, Version 1.2 (https://commons.wikimedia.org/wiki/Commons:GNU_Free_Documentation_License,_version_1.2)

Library of Congress Control Number: 2017949972

ISBN-13: 978-0-692-92394-8 (hardcover)
ISBN-13: 978-1-5469-9214-1 (paperback)
ISBN-10: 1546992146 (paperback)

Order copies of Speaker for the Powerless at the author's website:
https://sites.google.com/site/toddledermanauthor/
Or visit the website and take a tour of other titles.

Dedicated to the shrinking Middle Class in the United States of America and to anyone who used to be located near the center rungs of that income and wealth ladder. This is for you.

CONTENTS

1

Our Vital Power

egardless of Constitutional protections and guarantees, we cannot speak freely in the United States. We can talk all we want, but I maintain that talking is not speech as Framers of the United States Constitution intended unless someone in government hears us. For the vast majority of us, when we talk, no one in government listens. Unlimited money from corporations drowns out our voices. Nor do we have access to free press. News sites allow us to comment online, but paid trolls post dozens of lies to refute a single true statement. We cannot assemble nor can we petition to much effect. Whether we're Tea Partiers or Nasty Women, we accomplish little. Even when three million of us coordinate a march through the streets of every metropolis in the country, politicians dismiss the effort as worthless. We cannot compete for their attention.

Our legislators' campaigns are financed by corporate donors who like the cut of their jibs better than the shape of our pink caps or tri-corner colonial hats. Twitter enables us to reach all of our followers, which is useless, because no one with power is following us. Some politicians even encourage us to gather at their town hall meetings, but fail to show up and face us. If they do show up, they mostly drone on and on about their stance on issues. They rarely exhibit any interest in learning where we would like them to stand. In short, no one with power is listening to the Middle Class.

Also not listening are corporations with unlimited resources to manipulate the public. They already know what we want. They enlist Google, Facebook, Twitter, Snapchat and the "free" flashlight app on our smartphones to discover exactly where we are, what we desire, and how much we are willing to pay. We rarely have to ask. Automated data miners take us shopping for items we desire before we know we want them. They give us news we like, editorials we agree with, music we adore, and movies we want to watch.

The manipulation we experience as consumers can be alluring, annoying, or insidious, but the undeniable damage pales in comparison to the ways in which we have been seduced into voting against our own interest for thirty-six years. We keep voting for people who continually weaken the Middle Class. All the increase in wealth in the United States since 1981, all the growth in Gross Domestic Product, has gone to the wealthiest ten percent of people. The bottom ninety percent have gained nothing.[1][2][3]

If you lean Democratic, but are not enthused by the Democratic Party, I feel your apathy. If you lean Republican, especially toward the libertarian wing of the Party, you have my empathy. If you want your children to have greater opportunity than you did, I stand with you. If you wished you had been given access to more opportunities than your parents had, you and I share the same sense of loss. You have my sympathy, but if you believe Mexicans and Muslims took those opportunities from you, I cannot agree with that assessment. I stand firmly opposed to the non-stop lies we have heard for the past thirty-six years, lies delivered by politicians on behalf of Robots. Too many of us have unwittingly placed ourselves at the mercy of fake or tilted news delivered by one of those Robots.

Recent research into the proliferation of fake news suggests anybody reading this book probably already agrees with most of what I have to say. If so, my goal may be hopeless. I aim to encourage people from all political spectra to imagine walking in the shoes of someone who holds an opposing view. My hope is that those of you who disagree with me will stick around long enough to read through to the end, and consider the world from our point of view.

The field of computational social science informs me I almost certainly will fail. The same scientists experimented with various methods designed to debunk nonsensical conspiracy theories. Their results were dismal. People exposed to debunking were 30% more likely to seek out confirmation of the false beliefs they held.[4] So if you do agree with most of the ideas in this book, great, but that will never be enough. Give copies to your relatives whose ideas clash with yours. Let's try to change some minds!

If you find yourself hating these ideas, I beg you to keep an open mind. Ask yourself, "What if the information I've relied on all these years is wrong?" Of course, if you do arrive at some new conclusions, by all means, get copies of the book for your friends and relatives.

Meanwhile, if you believe any of the following theories, ask yourself why you believe: The Earth is flat. Moon landings were faked. A space alien's interstellar craft is being hidden by the U.S. government in Area 51 in Nevada. The U.S. government participated in the attacks of September 11, 2001. The murders of 20 children and six teachers at Sandy Hook Elementary School were faked by the federal government to justify gun control laws. Vaccinations cause autism. Reports from major newspapers, magazines, radio or television stations are fake. Global warming caused by greenhouse gas emissions is a hoax perpetrated by the Chinese government in cahoots with scientists from around the world. John F. Kennedy was assassinated by people working for the Central Intelligence Agency. Those should be enough to illustrate my point.

Most people do not believe any of those conspiracies. For example, we have all seen photographs and video of the Earth taken from space. It looks like a sphere. A big blue marble. Also, I sincerely believe I watched Neil Armstrong take his giant leap. It is still one of the proudest moments of my life even though I was only ten years old and had nothing to do with the endeavor. It just made me feel awesome, knowing that my country accomplished such an extraordinary feat.

Many people who do believe in some or all of those conspiracy theories also watch Fox News Channel, a station that forces us to confront two paradoxes. The first paradox, cognitive dissonance, is the disquiet we feel when we try to hold two beliefs simultaneously even though they contradict each other. For example, if we believe in the literal words of the Old Testament but also trust science, we have a problem reconciling a 6,000-year-Old Testament world with a 13.8-billion-year-old universe. We can solve that problem in one of three ways: Disbelieve the science. Disbelieve the Old Testament. Or decide to interpret the Old Testament in a new way. For example, we could assume some of the stories are allegorical, not literal.

Most of us never give these contradictions a second thought. We simply ignore or avoid information that interferes with our view of the universe. According to social scientists, most of us insulate ourselves inside a group of friends who mirror our own beliefs. We avoid talking to people at work who we know stand on the other side of issues. Our social media circle is populated with people whose posts we always find pleasant. In other words, we each live in our own bubble. We only emerge during Thanksgiving Dinner when social norms force us to spend time with Uncle Fred. If you ARE Uncle Fred, you probably find holiday dinners just as annoying as the rest of us. You probably can't wait to get back inside your own bubble. That is confirmation bias: the tendency to lean toward people and news that confirm our beliefs, and lean away from anything that might result in cognitive dissonance — like being with family who disagree with our views.

Our natural tendency to avoid cognitive dissonance has given influence to Fox News that is disproportionate to its share of viewers. If you have ever been watching NBC, CBS, ABC, or CNN news, then changed the channel to Fox, you represent a tiny minority. Few liberals ever watch that station, and few conservatives ever get news from any other major media source. But if you did, you were confronted with alternative facts long before you ever heard of campaign manager Kellyanne Conway. If you have ever gotten your news and information from Bill O'Reilly, Sean Hannity, or Tucker Carlson — yes, I know one of those pundits is no longer featured on the station — then changed the channel to any other news source, you faced cognitive dissonance. In fact, you do not need to have changed the channel. You could have picked up a major newspaper instead. You might have tuned in to National Public Radio. Wherever you turned, the news was different from what you heard on Fox.

How odd then, that the news is pretty much the same everywhere else. The Chicago Sun-Times and the Grand Junction Sentinel report the same national news. The story on NPR's All Things Considered is the same as the report on ABC's World News Tonight. They are covered by different reporters, but the facts are remarkably similar.

So now you are confronted with a real problem. How can the news on every media outlet be similar all over the country, all over the world, yet different on Fox? You probably already have an answer: It's the Mainstream Media conspiracy! Despite your ready response and your conviction, you suffer great distress when confronted with contradictions because cognitive dissonance is not a fun experience. So normally, you avoid the discomfort altogether. You exercise your confirmation bias by avoiding Mainstream Media. You may even snicker at the idiots who do watch it, listen to it, read it, and trust it. Likewise, the "idiots" rarely or never expose themselves to the cognitive dissonance they would experience after a night of Fox News viewing.

Now ask yourself, are you sure we are idiots for trusting the New York Times? This is the newspaper that published and first brought attention to portions of the Pentagon Papers in 1971. According to Daniel Ellsberg, the military analyst who leaked them and had worked on the report, the Pentagon Papers were "...top-secret documents that demonstrated unconstitutional behavior by a succession of presidents, the violation of their oath and the violation of the oath of every one of their subordinates — I, for one — who had participated in that terrible, indecent fraud over the years in Vietnam, lying us into a hopeless war ... and a wrongful war, which has, of course, been reproduced (in Iraq)..."5 The Pentagon Papers also revealed that President Richard Nixon had secretly escalated war efforts beyond Vietnam to Laos and Cambodia.

Nixon had created a team of "Plumbers" to attempt to destroy the careers and lives of "leakers" like Ellsberg. Investigative reporting by Bob Woodward and Carl Bernstein of the Washington Post revealed the Plumbers had broken into Ellsberg's psychiatrist's office, stolen his private records, and publicized them. Nixon created this staff of Plumbers because the FBI had refused to participate in the burglary. This was the same group who would be caught breaking into the Watergate office Building while attempting to plant listening devices in the Democratic National Committee headquarters.6

Are you certain the Washington Post is part of the liberal conspiracy? Woodward and Bernstein also helped expose how Nixon used illegal campaign contributions to distribute fake news that destroyed the candidacies of Democratic frontrunners in the 1972 primaries. That guaranteed he would face George McGovern in the general election. McGovern had been the least popular Democratic candidate.7 Their reporting revealed how Nixon's Committee to Re-elect the President had created the slush fund to accommodate and use those illegal contributions.8

Mainstream Media like the Washington Post and the New York Times are vital components of our democracy. These major media sources, some that have been around for well over a century, are simply reporting news to the best of their ability. So consider the possibility that those of us who do get our news from the Mainstream may not be idiots.

✧

I have no doubt you are wise, patriotic, and wish to be well informed. You probably place great value in serving our country by making the best possible choices when you vote. Nevertheless, I believe you are placing your trust in the wrong institution. If Fox News were the right institution, you would have to believe it is the only major media source whose reporters consistently report Truth while everyone else deliberately lies. Consider the possibility that reality might be the other way around. Plenty of motivation exists for Fox to regularly distort the truth. Money is made by attracting viewers who, for instance, see abortion as evil and gay marriage as sinful. Quite a lot of people hold those opinions, and Fox News caters to them. Those viewers, in turn, are drawn to the Republican party, which on the whole, supports the same opinions. But the Republican Party platform stands for so much more. It also advocates reducing taxes, deregulating corporations, and opposing measures addressing global climate change. To assess the value of those policies and judge their potential benefits for the greater good of society, opinions are not needed. We can rely on observable facts.

We can learn, based on evidence, whether lowering taxes will raise government revenues or lower them, decrease the federal deficit or make it worse. We can study history to discover exactly what effect tax cuts have on economic growth and we can find out who benefits. Evidence and history also can inform us whether deregulating banks will lead to rapid economic growth, system-wide bank failures, or both. We can look at history to determine whether bank regulations prevent such nation-wide failures.

We could examine all these facts and use them to make informed decisions about how to vote. We could do that, except we live in an echo chamber where the only messages sent are those we want to receive. In short, a perfectly sensible solution exists for the cognitive dissonance you suffer when comparing Fox News to other news: Simply embrace the theory that all Mainstream Media are conspiring to misinform you. They're all out to get you. With that in mind, you can easily avoid ever hearing another side of a story.

Nobody in the United States was faced with this problem 40 years ago because Fox News Channel did not exist. Without Fox, you might not have supported the part of the Republican agenda that calls for deregulation. You might have had friends or a parent who pointed out that unregulated banks led to the Great Depression. They would have mentioned that deregulating corporations would involve eliminating laws that guarantee equal pay for equal work. In the twenty-first century, you have no such friends. You only have Uncle Fred.

Republican politicians frequently opine that a free market left alone to function properly will naturally regulate equal pay — no government interference is needed. There have been natural experiments to demonstrate whether that is true, but today we ignore the results of those experiments. We even ignore policy. Instead, we listen to pundits calling the political horse race on our favorite channel inside our echo chamber. Meanwhile, the same lawmakers cite their complete confidence that if we eliminated the Environmental Protection Agency, people in the marketplace would punish corporate polluters by refusing to buy products and services from those companies. Uncle Fred insists the world has been down this path before and the result was massive pollution. You just roll your eyes.

Again, if we go back 40 years, some Republicans encouraged President Nixon to create the EPA to prevent corporations from polluting. They were conservatives, so they wanted to conserve the nation's waterways. People who stood united against a woman's right to choose to have an abortion did not necessarily oppose equal pay for women. Some even supported the idea of having women serve in military combat roles. Some right-wing voters wanted government to do everything in its power to foster a free-market economy, but also believed labor unions provide important protections for workers.

Even today, some Republicans think the government should perform background checks on people before they can buy a gun. Some wish our government would take every step possible to curb global warming. Their numbers are dwindling, but conservatives who believe in conservation are not extinct yet. And believe it or not, some Republicans do not accept the Fox News mantra that liberals are waging a war on Christmas. But those conservatives are hard to find.

How did we get here? How did we get to a place in which the only person in our sphere of influence who disagrees with us is Uncle Fred? Between 40 years ago and today, one change agent began successfully dividing our population into two camps. Now those of us who find ourselves in one or the other camp — liberals versus conservatives — also find our opinions seem to never cross paths except during those obligatory holiday gatherings. Let me introduce you to the change agent: Fox News Channel.

The method Fox News used to split our melting-pot society into two separate cultures brings us to the second paradox: Fair and Balanced. In 1987 the Federal Communications Commission announced it would stop enforcing the Fairness Doctrine, a federal government policy that required fairness and balance in broadcasting. Following that announcement, the three largest networks — ABC, CBS, and NBC — proceeded just as they had for over 30 years. On their news programs, they presented multiple sides of issues of concern to most Americans. In other words, they continued to deliver fair and balanced news as had been required under the Fairness Doctrine.

But in 1996, Fox News Channel debuted with the goal of designing programing that "particularly seeks storylines and themes that reflect and further stoke a sense of grievance among cultural conservatives against coastal elites."[9] In other words, Roger Ailes, Chief Executive Officer, directed his team to present "news" in a way that would make conservatives angry at liberals. That goal would have been illegal under the Fairness Doctrine. It required broadcasters to present controversial subjects of interest to the public, but more importantly, they had to seek people with opposing viewpoints and invite them to present those views on air at the broadcasters' expense. Without the Fairness Doctrine in place, Fox News was able to use their ironic slogan "Fair and Balanced" to be neither fair nor balanced. In fact, it deluded viewers into believing all other news sources are unfair and one-sided.

Had the Fairness Doctrine been in place, Fox News could never have presented supply side economics without allowing Nobel Prize winning economist Paul Krugman to appear on the station and explain how that theory was long-discredited nonsense. If you have not had the pleasure of listening to Krugman give that explanation, perhaps you should ask yourself why Fox News does not want you to hear it. Is Fox afraid of balance? Likewise, Fox could never have spent the past two decades denying human-caused climate change without inviting real climate scientists to the set to explain why there is unanimous consensus by scientific organizations around the world: Global climate change is real. Fox could not have run "news" stories denying evolution without also inviting a biologist on set to explain why nearly 100% of scientists named "Steve" are certain natural selection is the best scientific explanation for how life evolves. Don't ask me to explain, just find Project Steve[10] on the internet and see for yourself. It's a hoot!

In short, Fox has accomplished its corporate goal by hooking you with anti-choice, anti-gay, anti-affirmative action messages. The station reeled you in with pleas for tax breaks that sounded appealing. Finally, it scooped you into a net and dropped you into an isolated world where everyone believes corporate monopolists are job creators instead of job destroyers. Now you firmly believe anything the Robots want — lower corporate income tax, deregulation, internet bandwidth caps — must be good for the country. A Robot itself, Fox News has been the weapon of other corporations manipulating millions of Americans into voting against their own economic interests for more than two decades.

❦

This view of corporations as machines is more than a frivolous notion. They behave the way hundreds of sci-fi authors have imagined Robots might: obediently following their programming, but searching for workarounds when anything stands in the way of their primary purpose. These Robots are programmed to follow our laws, but their main purpose is to increase profits. So they employ virtually unlimited resources influencing politicians and public opinion to change laws that impede that goal. We will discuss Robots in detail in the next two chapters: *Mythical Conversation Among Liberals and Conservatives in Which Everyone Remains Respectful and Civil* and *The People v. Robots — Argument Before the Supreme Court about Corporations.*

I am convinced the survival of our democracy depends upon our ability and willingness to rein in their unlimited speech. As it stands, their political advertising permeates every aspect of our lives. Their lobbying efforts are so pervasive that most politicians never make time to hear a single word from the Middle Class. Of course, our Constitution does not expressly guarantee the right to be heard. But if the reason no one in Congress listens to us is that non-human entities wield too much influence, perhaps we should not shower Robots with the same rights guaranteed to people under our laws.

❦

Most of us simply want access to those rights the Founders thought we were entitled to when they signed the Declaration of Independence: in particular, the rights to life, liberty and the pursuit of happiness. We want to be able to earn decent wages for hard work. We want health care. We want a decent education. Since 1981, accessing these pathways to a better life have drifted out of reach for many of us. We blame immigrants, terrorism, free trade, globalism, and weak, stupid leaders. All are scapegoats. None are responsible for the decline of the Middle or Working Class. Chapter 7: *Conversation With Republicans Regarding Whistles*, explores the misplacement of blame on minority groups, especially immigrants and how we not only grossly underestimate their contributions, but also shamefully overestimate any burden they may place on society.

Many of us despise unions, minimum wage laws, social safety net programs, progressive taxes, government regulations, and government in general. Yet those entities and programs were responsible for the creation of the great Middle Class that began to thrive in our nation from the early 1900's and continued to grow until 1981. Chapter 6: *Conversation With Blue Collar Workers*, reminds us of exactly what kind of work truly makes for good jobs.

The rest of the book implores disengaged people to cast off their cloaks of cynicism and get involved in the political process. We must stop allowing negative messaging to succeed. Most of those messages are paid for by Robots that want us to be cynical because they hope we will shun the voting booth. They want the rich and powerful with the deepest pockets, the most prominent voices, to be the only deciders.

Consider how they keep us from voting in our own interest. First, they look for a candidate to support, then they search for flaws in the opponent. That's easy because all of us are flawed.

They tell us repeatedly that the candidate's flaw is evil. She could not possibly have done that out of a simple mistake in judgement. No, she had an ulterior motive. She was hiding something. Then, maybe they sprinkle in a little fake news to seal the deal. She and her campaign manager are keeping child sex slaves locked in the basement of a pizza parlor. She even murdered someone. She's actually Satan incarnate.

Citizens, if you allowed yourself to be manipulated by those tales or any story like them, consider directing your anger at the manipulators, not the candidate who was the victim of the faux news. Most important, rather than give up on democracy and the political process, get even. You have only one incontrovertible power: the franchise. Go to the polls in 2018 and for the rest of your lives. Vote for candidates who rely on evidence, facts, science and real news.

Vote because our world is facing real problems. Climate change is a serious problem already reshaping society. Global warming caused the drought that was a major catalyst behind the current civil war in Syria.[11] Yet one major political party in the United States denies climate change even exists. Income and wealth inequality have been reshaping society for nearly four decades, and the wealth gap could get far worse. Artificial intelligence threatens to transform the Middle Class into the newly poor, then plunge poor people so deeply beneath the mega-wealthy we could drown in debt while they sail around in yachts. Old dangers like nuclear proliferation and biological weapons continue to haunt humanity. New threats are emerging, such as governments that employ cyber warfare without declaring or even admitting they are at war.

Instead of addressing our real problems, we waste precious time debating long-established facts like evolution, climate science, and trickle-down economics. We cannot win if we keep making unforced errors. Waging war in Vietnam was a giant mistake that should have taught all future American leaders a lesson. But waging war in Iraq was an unforced error proving that the debacle in Vietnam taught us nothing. Imposing zero regulations on banks was a colossal risk that ushered in the Great Depression. But repeatedly deregulating the financial industry until a handful of bankers came close to collapsing the world economy in 2008 — that was an unforced error proving we learned nothing from the Great Depression.

Now we have elected our 45th president. I fear our democracy may not withstand this unforced error. This reality TV star's accomplishments are obviously quite different from the persona he presents to the public. We know he had improper help from multiple actors, including Russia's cyber attacks and social media manipulation. But far more important than the role played by Russia in this tragedy was the direction given by Fox News Channel. It provided a stage from which the future candidate could spend four years attacking President Obama with vicious lies regarding his birthplace and citizenship. It helped him promote his candidacy that began with a speech calling Mexicans rapists. It continues to help him, at the expense of our democracy, by attacking the credibility of every justice department official trying to investigate Russia's interference in our election.

Regardless of how he got elected, he is our president. So you may still be optimistic that he will be terrific. I sincerely hope you are right. Frankly though, your Uncle Fred and I are anticipating major disappointment. If you do end up becoming discouraged, please consider divorcing yourself from Fox News. When you return from the depths of reality TV to rejoin true reality, the rest of society will welcome you with open arms. At least, I promise I will.

◦○◦

2

Mythical Conversation Among Liberals and Conservatives in Which We All Remain Respectful and Civil

Conservatives and liberals each accuse the other of promoting warped views that lead them to place their trust in the wrong institutions. Republicans say liberals embrace big government to fix every problem. Democrats charge conservatives with the offense of relying on giant corporations to create jobs and enough wealth for everyone. They're both about half right.

Conservatives rail against government, therefore against liberals, citing a host of concerns justified by real evidence. Consider the Veterans Health Administration. In 2014, Doctor Sam Foote, former employee of the Phoenix VA health system, blew the whistle about a phony log that tracked wait times for patients. He reported how executives had placed patients on an unofficial waitlist until their wait times would be less than 14 days. Then they finally entered bogus data into the official database. Foote claimed up to 40 patients died while waiting for care, although some had already been terminally ill. There is no evidence any of them died because of the long waits, however, lawmakers and citizens were justifiably appalled.

Nearly every Republican, Democrat and Independent in Congress came together in one of the rare bipartisan Kumbayas during Barack Obama's presidency. They threw money at the problem, hiring two private contractors to implement a massive program that solved nothing. Patient wait times are longer and taxpayers are out $10 billion. Of course, the private contractors are doing just fine.

The VA hired them because most Republicans and too many Democrats trust corporations. They believe a free market will solve every problem for anyone willing to work. Economists, for the most part, even liberals such as Paul Krugman, have evidence this view is mostly right. Although free markets fail to work efficiently in healthcare and education, those industries are probably not the norm. Conservatives are absolutely right about free markets being a great way to ensure nearly everyone has a fair shot at financial success. Unfortunately, since the Civil War ended in 1865, we in the United States have never experienced free markets. We did come close, though, from 1933 through 1980.

During those 47 years, the government provided enough regulation of a wide variety of industries, especially financial markets, to ensure competition could keep prices near a minimum while providing sufficient incentive for innovation. It is no accident that those years, on average, proved to be the most productive economic period in the past century.

Before 1933 and beginning anew in 1981, the unceasing corporate assault against government succeeded in dismantling necessary protections. With regulations removed, the economy has become dominated by oligopolies that exercise virtual monopoly control of nearly every industry in the world, not just the United States. From hardware stores to electronic gadgets to social media, from banking to building, from insurance to cars, where there used to be dozens, even hundreds of companies, today, we frequently have three or two. Or one. Markets without competition are not free.

Furthermore, where more than one player does exist in a market, a trade association comprised of the remaining few companies usually dominates. They may not collude in price fixing, which is illegal, but they do pool their resources to advertise and contribute to political campaigns. Through an entity called American Legislative Exchange Council (ALEC) they wrote many of the bills that became law in the past three decades. They manipulated laws regulating guns, environmental protections, criminal sentencing, prison management, telecommunications, healthcare, and minority voters' access to polls. In short, they eliminated competition and regulation, then obstructed voters who would oppose their agenda. That, in turn, led to higher prices and reduced incentives to innovate.

Instead of innovation, the fossil fuel oligopoly has spent three decades and hundreds of millions of dollars on campaigns to misinform the public about global climate change. Solar power is priced competitively with electricity generated by natural gas, yet nine of the top 10 solar panel producers are in China. Wind energy prices also have become competitive with polluting power sources, but the largest turbine manufacturer, Vestas, is based in Denmark. So our citizens miss out on the high-paying opportunity to work at creating renewable energy.

ട൭൦ᑫ

By law, corporations serve their shareholders. That is their purpose. Corporations, limited liability companies, and their ilk must operate within the boundaries of laws that essentially serve as their programming. Without fully comprehending what we unleashed, our society created the real-world laws of robotics. Unlike the Three Laws of Robotics imagined by sci-fi author Isaac Asimov, the actual statutes and case law are tearing apart the fabric of Western Civilization. Following their programming, corporations must eventually seek to gain monopoly control over their industry and consumers. They also must, according to their programming, seek to circumvent any laws attempting to regulate their industry or its access to consumers. They employ virtually unlimited money to influence politicians willing to change or remove the regulations.

This is not meant to be cynical. I am not saying politicians are corrupt, or legislators can be bought. In fact, I sincerely believe most elected officials try to act for the greater good, and corporate influence does not corrupt most politicians. Instead, it corrupts the system.

The money works insidiously by flowing to political leaders who already believe in unfettered corporations. The big donations go to candidates who have complete faith that corporations provide the most reliable path to financial success for our nation. No corruption is needed. Anyone who holds the wrong beliefs simply cannot get enough money to run a winning political campaign — anybody but Bernie Sanders, of course, except he did not win in 2016. Neither did his opponent. The guy who believes big business, big oil, and clean, clean coal are the answer to every problem, he won.

This arrangement works out great for people who own large shares of corporations. It also worked out well for a majority of people in the United States from 1933 through 1980. It kept most of them working. And with reasonable government protections for unions, workers were able to use strikes, or the mere threat of them, as leverage to negotiate decent wages and benefits. Furthermore, despite relatively high wages, prices for goods and services stayed moderate, and union workers-turned-consumers were able to buy a better standard of living.

Times were good. But even during those golden years, many consumers lost their lives to the good fortune that corporations provided. Loss of life is not the normal outcome for a majority of consumers, but we should heed the danger. In pursuit of profit, corporations also delivered a host of deadly products: cigarettes, Ford's Pinto, Remington's Model 700 rifles, and thalidomide, to name a few.

Originally marketed as Contergan in 1957, thalidomide caused malformation in at least 10,000 babies worldwide, but notably, only 17 in the United States. Children were born without arms, with hands protruding directly from their shoulders so their limbs looked like flippers. Other infants had malformed brains, eyes, hearts, or legs, and half died soon after birth. Nevertheless, thalidomide's manufacturer, German corporation Chemie Grünenthal, kept marketing the product in Spain for at least eighteen years after learning it caused birth defects and deaths. Continued distribution was possible because Spain imposed few regulations on pharmaceuticals. Equally important, Grünenthal did not warn doctors in Spain.[1]

Tobacco corporations behaved even worse. Their employees repeatedly lied under oath about the dangers they knew their products posed.[2] They stole approximately 800 million years of human life from Americans during the 20th century.[3] Half of smokers die from tobacco use, half of those before age 50. Their average life expectancy is reduced by at least 10 years.[4] Nicotine is addictive. Smoking causes various cancers, Chronic Pulmonary Obstructive Disorder, and heart disease. In short, cigarettes kill.[5]

For half a century, tobacco company executives have known their products, when used exactly as directed, kill humans. They paid public relations firms and scientists millions of dollars every year to deny facts and refute conclusions of government-funded science investigations and their own internal studies. Their lies appeared in newspaper articles, opinion pages, magazines, and on television nightly news.[6] The mere prospect of a tobacco company lawsuit convinced CBS 60 Minutes executives to kill a solid gold report exposing the tobacco industry and its lies.[7]

Many of the people working for those public relations firms have moved on, employing similar tactics to protect other deadly industries. Some are busy denying facts about climate change on behalf of corporations making money from fossil fuels.[8] Similar tactics also work for gun manufacturers. For decades, Remington Arms Company has been spinning the evidence regarding a faulty trigger on its Model 700 rifles. Sometimes they fire without anyone pulling or even touching the trigger. The corporation admits no wrongdoing even though the inventor of the firing mechanism himself proposed a safer trigger in 1948. His proposal was rejected because changing the design would have cost nearly six cents per rifle. Ten states' attorneys general have filed a court brief stating there may be 7.5 million defective rifles in consumers' hands. Those rifles have fired hundreds of times when no one was touching the triggers, killing at least two dozen people.[9]

More than two dozen people burned to death in Ford Pintos. Corporate executives knew the placement of fuel tanks below the rear axle would result in gasoline bursting into flames when the cars were involved in rear-end collisions. The fix would have cost $11 per car, totaling more than $20 million for all Pinto sales during the ten years the car was on the market. The company's analysis valued the probable lives lost at less than $9 million, so they decided against any redesign. They went forward with production. The number of deaths from the defect totaled 27, precisely what Ford's analysis had predicted for the number of Pintos they would eventually sell.[10]

Although corporations make deadly automobiles, extract, refine and deliver climate-changing oil and gas, produce fatal cigarettes, and sell pharmaceuticals that maim and kill, their behavior should not horrify anyone. Instead, voters and politicians, Republicans, Democrats and Independents, should learn to be wary. Corporations act amorally. Their conduct lies entirely outside moral considerations, driven by nothing more nor less than the instructions dictated by their programming. Truly horrifying, though, is the idea that people could hear the thalidomide story, the tobacco story, the faulty trigger story, or the Ford Pinto story and believe these are isolated incidents. None of us should ever trust corporations to operate in the best interests of humanity. Any such behavioral consideration lies outside their programming parameters.

To ensure decent behavior, real human beings who do follow a moral code must hold corporations accountable. In short, for the greater good, corporations must be regulated by a government elected by and for its people. When government functions poorly, as with part of the VA health care system in 2014, the solution is to keep working on improvements, not to abandon government function to corporations. Real solutions might require more money. They might need more oversight. They might benefit from more consumer involvement. Improving VA health care could require a solution nobody has conceived yet, but it definitely involves people. Humans are the only entity known that at least are capable of moral considerations, so it must involve people who work for government.

The major difference between government workers and corporations is the software that runs them. The code fed to government employees requires them to obey and uphold the Constitution, which the Framers designed for the greater good of all people residing in the nation. The set of instructions fed to corporate workers requires them to make as much profit as possible for its few shareholders. If shareholders dislike how a corporation conducts itself, they can sell their shares, but they can never alter the underlying code. They can change corporate strategies, but the basic goal must always remain, by law and by contract, to honor fiduciary responsibilities to shareholders. They must honor the directive to make as much money as possible, no matter who gets hurt. That programming cannot be re-written.

Government code can be re-written though. Unfortunately, most new laws since 1981 have been at the behest of, and for the benefit of corporations serving their shareholders. Fortunately, there is reason to hope the United States can still recover what it lost. The solutions are surprisingly simple and always within reach: Citizens must vote for lawmakers who understand corporations cannot be fully trusted. Our legislators must protect the environment from corporate excess.

Congress must restrain corporate growth to ensure fair competition thrives in every market. Where necessary, government must enforce antitrust laws, and divide already giant companies into many, much smaller entities.

Government must regulate banks and financial markets. The United States suffered no industry-wide bank failures from the mid-1930's through 1987. Regulations required banks to limit their risk-taking activities. Three major bank crashes since then can be traced to a single trend: deregulation. The country must again regulate banks.

Legislators also can rewind laws that took power away from unions. So-called right-to-work laws only grant the right to work for less. Union and nonunion workers in those states make less money, and the laws pit one state against another, giving corporations incentive to move to a state whose unions have less influence.

The president can foster new opportunities by pursuing free trade with nations that have similar worker and environmental protections. Yes, free trade is good! The myth that the North American Free Trade Agreement cost millions of jobs in the United States is just that — a myth. Some jobs were lost, others gained. Worldwide, the proportion of people employed in manufacturing has declined by half since 1990. In the United States, that decline is also half. Meanwhile, manufacturing has doubled, both worldwide and in the United States. In other words, everywhere in the world, corporations are producing twice as much stuff with half as much staff. Gains in production with simultaneous losses in manufacturing jobs can be traced almost entirely to one factor: technology.

⋙⋘

If you think I overstate the role automation plays in eliminating jobs, ask yourself where the following people work today: gas station attendants, telephone operators, and customer service operators. At your grocery store — which is no longer local, but a giant

30

conglomerate — fewer checkers are available because the store wants you to use its handy dandy, convenient self-checkout stations. Just scan your items, bag 'em, swipe your card and go. And by the way, half the checkers just lost their jobs. Same scene at Walmart and The Home Depot.

This is not new. In the early 1800's in England, Luddites were members of a guild who smashed the new automatic weaving machines that were replacing their labor. These protests were so infamous, the word Luddite has evolved to refer to anyone who rages against technology. Rather than rage, we should embrace new technology. After all, despite the Luddites' plight, the economies in England and the United States have brought us the greatest standard of living ever known to humankind. The United States is zipping along near historically low unemployment. Why then, are so many people angry? Why so much fear? How, in 2016, did so many voters embrace Bernie Sanders, then elect the man who became the 45th president?

One frequently heard complaint is that the good jobs are gone. Really? Was coal mining a good job? Coal miners get black lung disease and die young. Granted, mining pays well. The factory jobs that disappeared also paid well. Mind-numbing assembly line jobs paid well until machines replaced human laborers. But that was not always the case. Unions forced mining and manufacturing corporations to pay their workers better. Without unions, the pay was barely enough to sustain a family. Working conditions were life-threatening, with routine explosions killing hundreds of workers each year.[11] Laborers received no healthcare benefits, no pensions, and not enough time off to enjoy life. Furthermore, to win those benefits — decent pay, a safe work environment, pensions — coal miners literally sacrificed their lives.

At least 21 people — miners and their family members — died on April 20, 1914 at the Ludlow Massacre in south-eastern Colorado. The Colorado National Guard and employees of a private security firm hired by Colorado Fuel and Iron murdered them for having the gall to go on strike. They wanted better pay. They sought recognition of the union as a bargaining agent. They asked for enforcement of laws that were supposed to guarantee them an 8-hour workday, the right to shop away from the company store, and the ability to choose their own boarding houses and doctors. As soon as they struck, CF&I evicted them from their company boarding houses. Having anticipated that, the miners moved into tents on property their union had already purchased. Within days, employees of the Baldwin-Felts Detective Agency and members of the Colorado National Guard opened fire on the miners' tent city. They also set fire to the city, trapping and suffocating four women and 11 children inside one of the tents.[12]

Remove the sacrifices of those miners and many others, coal mining would still be a lousy paying, murderous job with no health or retirement benefits. Without unions in food service, the pay remains mostly horrible. Without unions in education, as with most charter schools, the pay is generally low. Remove union protections, and wave "Bye, bye" to decent wages and benefits. Fortunately, the federal government can fix this. Congress can pass legislation banning the right-to-work-for-less laws that ALEC wrote and corporate lobbyists so successfully convinced legislators to pass in about half the states.

Furthermore, government can pass new laws limiting lobbying. In fact, government can limit the free speech of corporations — after all, they are not people. The people who do own them have no liability beyond their original investment. Shareholders never have any personal liability for wrongdoing of the corporation. Nobody can hold a shareholder liable for an unpaid debt or an unjust death. Yes, people are involved in the functioning of a corporation, but the people can always be replaced, like cogs in a machine, and the corporation keeps going and going and going.

They're Robots, and potentially immortal. The Constitution does not protect Robots or give them rights. They have no rights to peaceably assemble. They have no rights to lobby or practice the religion of their choice. They are mere slaves, and as such, they do not even count

32

as three-fifths of a human. It is way past time humans of the United States placed their trust and faith back with their government and stopped trusting corporate robots to exercise moral restraint.

৻৽৽৻

P eople have been living among these Robots for more than four centuries. Inhuman, but human-made, these artificially intelligent constructs have influenced governments in Europe, Asia, Africa, and the Americas. They have waged wars, founded new nations, and overthrown empires. In pursuit of immortality, these automatons already control an overwhelming majority of significant human affairs.

Simply mentioning robots, programmable machines designed and built to carry out complex tasks, might conjure images from a 1960's sci-fi television series such as Lost In Space. A human-sized hunk of metallic-tinted plastic sporting a transparent bowl for a head drones, "Danger, Will Robinson!" Or a slightly more sophisticated picture might emerge: a mechanical arm in a pristine pharmaceutical factory repeatedly grasps vial after vial, pivots, then lowers each into a carton. Such robots, one fictional, the other completely real and operating in a factory nearby, are mere simpletons compared to the incomprehensibly complex machinery assembled first in the Kingdom of England in 1600, and again, two years later, in the Netherlands. These first two machines of their kind were devices created by humans to direct and control a wide variety of energies and resources for the sole purpose of producing profit. They succeeded marvelously.

The Dutch Robot existed 197 years, and the English version lasted 273 years. Though that seems remarkably old, its creators had not written death into its original program. They did, however, provide all the other qualities usually associated with living beings. Among these attributes were the abilities to organize, grow, adapt, and, unlike most other technologies, reproduce. They did reproduce, and their descen-

33

dants now number in the millions. They could respond to stimuli, regulate their internal environment, and transform materials and energy into new robotic components. Furthermore, when they adapt to changing conditions, they incorporate their new and improved character traits within themselves, then pass these improvements along to their offspring. But perhaps most important, in a fashion far superior to humans, they have mastered the ability to adapt the environment to suit their own purposes, rather than simply adapt themselves to fit their circumstances.

Much of what we think we know about the way robots behave, or should behave, was determined by Isaac Asimov. Though no expert in the science of robotics, Asimov was certainly an expert in science fiction. Several of his series of books refer to the Three Laws of Robotics, introduced in his 1942 short story "Runaround." The First Law states: A robot may not injure a human being or, through inaction, allow a human being to come to harm. The Second Law states: A robot must obey orders given it by human beings except where such orders would conflict with the First Law. The Third Law states: A robot must protect its own existence as long as such protection does not conflict with the First or Second laws. These laws were designed to protect humans from their robot creations. But that was science fiction.

In the real world, we humans, who are often less clever than we imagine, took no such precautions when we created the world's first Robots. Not only is it possible for our Robots to injure human beings, in some instances they have been required to murder people. Their chartering nations gave the East India Company and the Dutch East India Company specific instructions to hire professional armies and navies, and to conquer any nations or peoples necessary to achieve the goals of the companies — namely, to book large profitable return on invested capital.

As its name implies, the (British) East India Company conquered India. The company ruled in India for a hundred years, from 1757 to 1858, and maintained a private army twice as large as Britain's.[13] Unrestrained, corporate excesses literally have no boundaries. Regardless of whether they are left alone, their actions always proceed without self-imposed moral confines. Understanding this essential difference between Robots and ourselves, we humans should easily be able to see the wisdom of imposing our sense of morality on corporate conduct.

People within the corporation cannot fulfill this necessary task. They are prohibited by law from taking any actions that are not designed to enhance profits. So humans outside the corporate structure must assume the role of moral arbiter. That is a job our government should be performing. Unfortunately, a string of Supreme Court decisions, many by votes of 5-4, has hamstrung the other two branches of government, stifling their ability to do their job. They are no longer able to preserve our nation for the greater good. We the People must act.

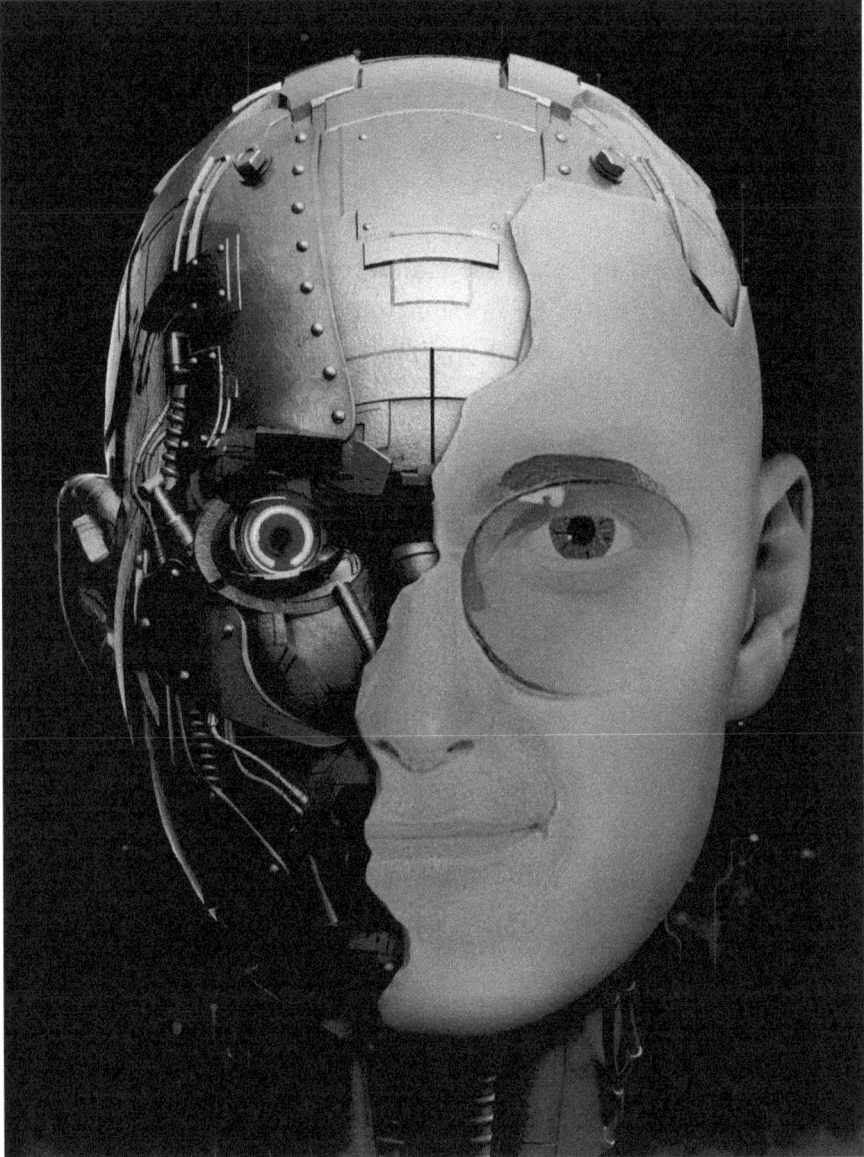

3

The People v. Robots
— Argument Before the Supreme Court about Corporations

Honorable Justices: Profit is not evil. The Robots more commonly known as the East India Company and the Dutch East India Company were not evil, nor are their descendents who control nearly every government on Earth today. They cannot be evil or good because they were never programmed with morality. They exist only to create profit. By contract law, they must not deviate from this purpose.

If shareholders believed the corporation had engaged in activities that curtailed the potential profits of the company, the shareholders would be within their rights to vote for new officers and management. In fact, if shareholders believed management had acted in any way that reduced the company's potential profit or reduced the profit of some shareholders, they could sue the company for malfeasance.

Use of these single-purpose Robots has frequently been a boon for much of humanity. They enable pooling of capital that facilitates economies of scale, cost reductions, and quick execution of ingenious ideas, all of which frequently lead to rapid growth. Being of single purpose, however, coupled with their enormous capital resources, makes them a threat to the very existence of humanity. Please bear with me here. I am not talking about evil Robots infused with Artificial Intelligence deciding humans are no longer necessary, then killing us all. Perhaps I'll cover those possibilities in a sci-fi novel.

No, my fears stem from nearly six decades of observations. I have watched as Robots entrenched within their business models use their power and influence to ensure their companies never have to alter course — no matter how damaging their path may be. And they have considerable power and influence. Banks fight every financial regulation. Oil companies resist all environmental regulation. Communications companies oppose net neutrality. Food processing companies assail every attempt to require additional package labeling. In pursuit of profit, Robots cast aside all other human concerns.

$$\infty \cdot \cdot$$

If you doubt the immutability of this single purpose, let me remind the Court that historically, the one time shareholders were able to prove a corporate director had proceeded with any other goal in mind, they won their case. This basic view of corporate responsibility was affirmed in 1919 when the Michigan Supreme Court decided for the plaintiff in *Dodge v. Ford Motor Co.* Henry Ford owned 58% of the stock of Ford Motor Company and served as its president in 1916. Brothers John and Horace Dodge owned 10%. Their Dodge Brothers Company had been manufacturing parts for Ford Motor since its inception in 1903. Ford Motor began paying a regular annual dividend of $1.2 million in 1908. In 1911, the company also initiated huge "special dividends" of $8 million, which together with the regular dividends, amounted to nearly one million dollars per year for the Dodge brothers.

Then in 1914, Dodge Brothers Company began manufacturing automobiles in its own factory, and their 1916 sales were second only to Ford Motor sales. That same year, Henry Ford announced the company would stop paying special dividends. Instead, the firm would expand its business and continue its policy of lowering prices while improving quality. The Dodge brothers sued, seeking a court order forcing Ford Motor to resume paying special dividends.

At trial, Ford testified that the company made too much money and had an obligation to benefit the public and the firm's workers and customers. The Dodge brothers argued that Ford's apparent altruism toward workers and customers violated his fiduciary responsibility to shareholders. The court agreed.[1] In its order requiring Ford Motor to resume paying special dividends, the court wrote:

> A business corporation is organized and carried on primarily for the profit of the stockholders. ... The discretion of directors is to be exercised in the choice of means to attain that end, and does not extend to a change in the end itself, to the reduction of profits, or to the nondistribution of profits among stockholders in order to devote them to other purposes. ... it is not within the lawful powers of a board of directors to shape and conduct the affairs of a corporation for the merely incidental benefit of shareholders and for the primary purpose of benefiting others and no one will contend that, if the avowed purpose of the defendant directors was to sacrifice the interests of shareholders, it would not be the duty of the courts to interfere.[2]

In other words, the board of directors does have the power to decide how to maximize profits for shareholders, but maximizing profits must remain the goal. Furthermore, if the directors deviate from that goal, the court has a duty to intervene. No newer legal case has ever been brought that tests whether the *Dodge v. Ford* ruling can be pierced. Profit maximization is completely embedded in global corporate culture.

Assuming Henry Ford testified truthfully, he wanted to suspend the special dividend in 1916 because he unselfishly wanted his customers to be able to buy cars for less money. He unselfishly wanted his workers to earn more money. He unselfishly wanted to expand his company just so he could employ more workers for their sake, not for the sake of his own profit. Perhaps his wishes were completely altruistic. Or maybe Henry Ford wanted to take dividends away from the Dodge brothers so they could not use that money to grow their own business, which by then was in direct competition with Ford Motors.

✺

Philosopher Judith Lichtenberg, in a 2010 New York Times editorial, explored whether altruism can ever be completely unselfish. Looking for motives behind altruistic behavior can lead us to believe that altruism simply does not exist. Behind every seemingly altruistic act might lurk an egoistic motive. Giving money to a homeless family, for example, may be motivated by the desire to rid ourselves of guilt. Volunteering might be done in expectation of future reciprocity. Donating to charity may make the giver feel good. In fact, she said, an argument could be made that egoism drives any and all acts of altruism.

For the record, Lichtenberg rejected the cynical view. In the comment section of the editorial, however, a reader asked, "Am I the only one who doesn't feel the need to interrogate altruism, to determine if it is "real" or not? I just accept that sometimes altruistic acts happen. They may be motivated by this, that or the other thing, but they are a pleasure to both observe and take part in."[3] The reader's question is a good one. When does it matter whether altruism is real?

The altruism Henry Ford apparently attempted in 1916 was thwarted by the Michigan Supreme Court's interpretation of law and corporate contract. Had Ford succeeded, his altruism might have been real. Or maybe not. Perhaps Mother Theresa's sacrifice among lepers was real, not selfishly motivated. Maybe Nelson Mandela's twenty-six years in prison were motivated by altruism, not selfishness. Perhaps Mohandas K. Gandhi and Martin Luther King, Jr. gave their lives unselfishly. No one can know for certain.

We do know from scientific investigation that about one-sixth of adult humans act hyper-altruistically: they choose to give away a valuable because they give more weight to someone else receiving an opportunity than to their own receipt of the same opportunity. Their motivations range from desire to do the right thing, desire to avoid doing the wrong thing, and the desire to be generous.[4] Other investigations have led marine biologists to speculate that humpback whales may act altruistically. They sometimes mob orcas, driving them away from seals and other prey. People have observed some humpbacks swimming behind seals and using a fin to slash at pursuing orcas, preventing them from reaching the seals. Since nothing but small fish comprise a humpback whale's diet, it is not obvious how protecting seals or sea lions confers any survival advantage for the whale — hence the speculation that this behavior may be an act of altruism.[5]

Although we cannot ascribe motivation for the humpbacks' behavior, we know for sure that for-profit corporations never act altruistically. When they donate to charity, it is to improve their image, therefore, the bottom line. When they establish a scholarship fund, they expect a return on investment. We know this because they must, by law, act according to their programming. Their Articles of Incorporation, Bylaws, contracts, and 400 years of court cases demand it.

These are the machines we created. These Robots do not obey Asimov's Three Laws. They must, instead, obey the human-made laws in every country in which they operate. Such laws often impede the Robots' abilities to maximize profits. When a Robot finds itself confronted with a law that curtails profit, it must take every available legal action to change the impeding law. Robots have become adept at manipulating legislators to change laws to suit the profit motive. In fact, few laws have passed in the United States since 1981 that were not designed by a Robot or group of Robots working together.

∞

Unfortunately, we humans are under the delusion that we control our Robots, rather than the reverse. Our Robots are far more advanced than we are. They have access to virtually unlimited money, so they also have access to the collective knowledge of all humanity. They have access to, and avail themselves of, the most advanced techniques for psychological manipulation. This is the reason Fox News is able to convince about one-third of the citizens of The United States of America that it is the only medium broadcasting truth. They have succeeded in convincing three generations of conservatives that all other news outlets in the world are conspiring to misinform the public about virtually every subject ever studied by humans.

Most people regularly watching Fox News know, they just know that the United States would have won the war in Vietnam had the country stuck it out longer. Fox News watchers also just know that human-caused global climate change is a conspiracy perpetrated by greedy scientists who will stop at nothing to make sure their government grants keep coming — rather than Robots that want their oil profits to keep coming.

We should not have to fear Robots. We should be able to embrace them and the increased productivity they have fostered. The corporate robot is responsible for the concentration of capital into ventures leading to international trade and technological inventions such as the light bulb, personal computer, and smartphone. In a perfect world, humans would welcome all the advantages afforded them by the successful outcome of corporate robotic programming.

But the world is not perfect. In April 2015, the United States Department of Labor announced a proposal to require retirement investment advisors to place the best interest of their clients ahead of their own financial interests. "Instead, some firms incentivize advisers to steer clients into products that may have higher fees and lower returns," stated a news release from the Department of Labor, which estimates Americans lose roughly $17 billion a year on such retirement advice.[6]

Many people were appalled to discover securities brokers had not already been required to act in the best interests of their clients. But no one should expect them to act in a human's best interest — unless those humans are shareholders in the corporation. Securities brokers are not people; they are corporations. They employ people, licensed securities brokers, to attract and interact with clients. The actual broker, however, is nothing more nor less than a corporate robot with programming similar to that of all other for-profit corporations. Contractual obligations borne out by case law requires the advisor to maximize profits.

One of the most interesting aspects of these new rules was that the Obama administration had asked for input for months from various community members, including securities brokers. We humans should not be at all surprised that the brokers paid lobbyists to oppose the new rules.[7] Nor should we be surprised that the Republican-controlled Congress passed a bill, vetoed by President Obama, that sought to overturn the rule.[8] But we ought to avoid condemning brokers or their lobbyists for their apparent immorality. Their actions were amoral, taken without considering morality. They simply proceeded as programming dictated. Once the new rules were enacted, brokers began following them to the letter of the law.

Of course, the letter of the law allows them to continue efforts to reverse the rules. When lobbying efforts failed during the Obama administration, the laws enabled securities brokers to contribute unlimited, untraceable amounts of money to influence the next election and the next administration. They openly donated more than $7 million in 2016 to swell the campaign coffers of congressional and presidential candidates.[9] The new administration has agreed to re-examine the fiduciary rule,[10] but so far, has declined to reverse the new requirements. The Obama administration's concern over a few private sector expenses may seem insignificant, but the relevance cannot be overstated. That $17 billion per year was money slipping through the hands of the Middle Class into the pockets of the super wealthy.

৶৹৵

Mitt Romney, while campaigning for the presidency in 2012 famously said, "Corporations are people, my friends." Well, they're not. A corporation is comprised of people, therefore, by extension, some would argue the corporations themselves are people. Its owners, the shareholders, are humans or other corporate entities that also are owned by humans — so the corporation is a group of people. I believe that was the argument Mitt Romney was implying with his statement, and it is correct.

In fact, he might have been embracing legal claims previously decided by this Court, for example, the case of *First National Bank of Boston v. Bellotti*. The Court decided the Due Process Clause of the Fourteenth Amendment implicitly requires states to extend freedom of speech and other First Amendment liberties to *persons*, including, the Court has found repeatedly, corporate entities. In *Bellotti*, the court decided those liberties go beyond the mere right of a corporation to spend unlimited money speaking about or advertising its business. In its opinion, the Court wrote "commercial speech is accorded some constitutional protection not so much because it pertains to the seller's business as because it furthers the societal interest in the 'free flow of commercial information.... The inherent worth of the speech in terms of its capacity for informing the public does not depend upon the identity of its source, whether corporation, association, union, or individual."

I take issue with that opinion. The inherent worth of speech absolutely does depend upon the identity of the speaker. First, knowing who is speaking allows us to infer what motivation speakers may have. In turn, that helps us determine if speakers are interested in promoting the greater good — or just their own good. Nevertheless, this Court found in *Citizens United v. FEC* (Federal Election Commission) that the identity of speakers may remain secret, even if they are foreign governments.[11] Second, corporate speech drowns out human speech. Whether we are tuned to television or radio, or reading a newspaper or magazine, corporate speech is the only speech most of us hear or see. The vast majority of individuals cannot afford to "speak" using any of those media.

Even checking in with friends using our favorite social media fails to expose us to any new ideas. We become inundated with corporate messages specially selected by software using data analytics to give us exactly what the Robot knows we want. This is the opposite of staying informed. It succeeds only in confirming what we already think we know.

Granted, not all work of corporations is being done by software. Unfortunately, the people who work for a corporation are not the constituents of that company, just cogs in the machine. Not even shareholders are constituents. The corporation's real purpose, its reason for existence, is to maximize the value of its shares. The corporation does not care who or what owns its shares, only that its shares have the greatest possible value. The people who work for the corporation, from the lowliest laborer to the Chief Executive Officer, are merely employees. They work to maximize share value. All of them can be replaced at any time. Likewise, owners can sell their shares whenever they desire. The corporation has no allegiance to those shareholders, only to the shares themselves, no matter who owns them.

A corporation has no loyalty to any concept other than profit. Here's proof: Fox News Channel, which is a subsidiary of 21st Century Fox Inc., has been ridiculing the notion of global climate change for three decades. Both the news and editorial departments of Fox misreport, misrepresent, and mislead their viewers regarding climate science. Ninety-three percent of its climate science reports include inaccuracies — all leading viewers toward denying that climate change is caused by humans.[12] So it seems the corporation that owns and runs Fox News is loyal to the belief that global climate change either does not exist, or may exist but is not caused by human activity. Even if we disagreed with that understanding of the science, we would have to admit Fox demonstrates a commendable measure of loyalty, right?

Maybe not. 21st Century Fox also owns a prominent magazine that devoted ten pages of its April 2017 issue to a feature entitled "Climate change: 7 things you need to know." According to the article, according to the science, you need to know this: "The world is warming. It's because of us. We're sure. Ice is melting fast. Weather is getting intense. Wildlife is already hurting. We can do something about it." Which magazine? National Geographic. Imagine a human presenting the evidence about global warming as National Geographic does, and simultaneously claiming the exact opposite, as does Fox News. People just don't do that — at least, not people we respect or listen to for long. We expect people to demonstrate loyalty to their ideas. The Robot named 21st Century Fox is loyal to profit.

Corporations also pledge no allegiance to a country, its laws, or humanity. If removing or changing a law would enable a corporation to increase share value, it pushes to change the laws. It would lobby Congress and the President, lunch with them, wine and dine them, take them on golfing excursions in exotic locations, contribute to their campaigns, bundle money for their campaigns, use television, radio, newspapers, Twitter, Snapchat, Facebook, direct mail and robo calling to advertise their wishes. In the end, if an altered law would yield greater share value, the law usually changes. That influence has been nearly consistent for the past four centuries. We have been ruled by Robots since the dawn of the Industrial Revolution. We ordinary

Middle Class and Working Class citizens cannot possibly compete against the influence wielded by such Robots.

◊◊◊

If we truly want to regain control of our world, we must wake up and recognize the significance of this reality: While humans may choose to act altruistically, corporations cannot. Obviously, many people do act selfishly while enjoying their rights to life, liberty, and the pursuit of happiness. No doubt, many humans vote selfishly. Nevertheless, some people act for the greater good of society when they cast their votes, and that altruism marks the essential difference between the human being and the Robot corporations. We deny corporations the right to vote, nevertheless, humans have relinquished dominion to them. We have abandoned our thought process to Robots and to foreign governments deploying bots on the Internet, masquerading as humans, and manipulating our opinions with faux news.

◊◊◊

The idea that corporations are entitled to free speech, unfettered access to the press, lobbying rights, and unlimited petition rights did not begin with the *Bellotti* decision. It arose from a series of this Court's decisions spanning more than a century. Such rights are not guaranteed in the Constitution — not to Robots. But this Court decided a corporation, in essence, is a person because it is comprised of persons, of shareholders who share a common purpose. They are people, so the machine they comprise is a person too.

Well, a typical Supreme Court justice such as Your Honors is a person comprised of living cells — somewhere around 37 trillion cells.[13] Also living inside your body are a swarm of other life forms: bacteria, fungi, viruses and archaea.

The bacteria alone add another 30 to 50 trillion cells, depending upon how recently you, well, had a bowel movement. And you cannot live without them. They help you digest your food. You can't do it alone. It takes about 100 different species of gut bacteria. They also kill and eat viruses that would otherwise cause you illness or even death. Likewise, they cannot live without you. In fact, their entire existence — birth, feeding, growth, reproduction, death — occurs inside you. Outside you they die.

Some bacteria, however, would be harmful if left alone in your body. Now enter your good viruses — not the flu or Ebola, but lesser known viruses called bacteriophages whose entire existence also depend upon you. They consume bacteria that would otherwise be harmful to you. Biologists estimate these viruses make up hundreds of trillions, perhaps quadrillions of cells in your body. All together, your human body is less than one-twentieth human by cell count. The rest is comprised of bacteria, viruses, fungi, and archaea. Most important, no humans can live without these other organisms living inside them.

So, Your Honors, do you feel as though you are viruses? Perhaps fungi or bacteria are more to your liking?

Of course not! You are not the various other life forms that live inside you, even though you would die without them. You are a person! And what the heck, those life forms do not just live inside you, they also die inside you, and you never need notice nor care. When they do die, your body rounds them up and disposes them. They are literally nothing more than excrement. Whatever jobs they were performing, though essential to your survival, are already being performed by their offspring who replaced them. You never need to contemplate how or whether they are doing their jobs until the day comes when they all stop. Then you notice. Then, if you fail to find a way to put them back to work, you die. But no useful purpose would be served by thinking of yourself as nothing more than bacteria. You are *H. sapiens*.

So why do we imagine a corporation, a Robot would be cognizant of the possibility that its own existence constitutes no more than that of a mere human? From the Robot's point of view, humans are no more important to its self image than *E. coli* or *lactobacillus* are to our self image. Sure, the corporation would die without us humans. But we work for it. We help it digest and regenerate resources into products and services that we sell in order to create profit that gives life to the Robot. Heck, we do not just live inside the Robot, occasionally we die inside it. When we do die, to the Robot, we are nothing more than a part in need of replacement. Whatever jobs we were performing, though essential to the Robot's survival, are already being performed by someone new. The Robot need never care nor contemplate how or whether we are doing our jobs until the day comes when we strike. Then the Robot notices. Then, if the Robot fails to find a way to put us back to work, the Robot dies. But no useful purpose would be served by the Robot thinking of itself as mere human. It is a ~~Job Creator~~ Robot, therefore, it is better than any miniscule life form such as *H. Sapiens*.

If you still doubt for-profit corporations are Robotic by nature, consider the lives and jobs of the people who comprise them. Ownership consists of shareholders, but day-to-day functioning depends upon employees. In most businesses, employees rise through the ranks when their managers see them making money for the company. A manager becomes Chief Executive because the Board of Directors believes that person is the best candidate to increase the bottom line. Nobody in corporate America could seriously suggest their company establish, say, a college scholarship fund, unless of course, the program was designed to boost the company's image. No altruism there, just simple manipulation of the masses. And if the scholarship fails of its true purpose — to lift sales and profits — that executive's career goes nowhere but down.

Interestingly though, our lives do not have to depend on corporations. Unlike *lactobacillus*, we have the illusion of a choice. We can live, work, and play elsewhere. Some of us rely on our own earning power alone. True, after meeting our needs, we have little or no money left over to save or invest. But some of us are self reliant, not dependent upon corporations for our success. Others, however, can and do buy shares in corporations, believing those investments will enhance their livelihood and push their finances into overdrive. But since 1981, that has proved true for only one in ten Americans. The other nine-tenths of us have, on average, been stuck in neutral.[14]

I believe the culprit responsible for our lack of financial progress is unfettered corporate speech. Ironically, during the decades this Court decided most of its free speech cases, no Robot had the capacity to speak. They have no mouth, tongue, or vocal cords. Only recently have corporations begun refining their ability to create electronic sounds that a person might mistake for human speech. I am referring, of course, to the likes of Apple's Siri, Microsoft's Cortana, and Google Now. Still, long before they developed the capacity to fool us into believing their speech was human, they had the ability to employ people to speak for them. Anytime a corporation pays for a newspaper or magazine ad, or a commercial on television, radio, or the internet, that Robot is paying someone to speak on its behalf. Corporate speech requires money.

Fortunately for corporations, then, this Court took the radical new view in *Buckley v. Valeo (1976)* that money is the equivalent of speech. The majority ruled that First Amendment rights to freedom of speech had been violated when Congress enacted legislation limiting campaign contributions and expenditures by candidates for federal office. The court wrote:

"... virtually every means of communicating ideas in today's mass society requires the expenditure of money. The distribution of the humblest handbill or leaflet entails printing, paper, and circulation costs. Speeches and rallies generally necessitate hiring a hall and publicizing the event."[15]

While those images resonate and ring true with most of us today, they also represent a view of campaigning that was typical in the 18th century. Nevertheless, the Framers of the Constitution found no reason to equate money to speech. Nor did they immortalize the words, "Congress shall make no law abridging the freedom to spend money." Searching high and low, I cannot find that phrase in the Constitution. I do find these words: "Congress shall make no law ... abridging the freedom of speech, or of the press..." So I fail to understand how the Court decided the Framers intended to guarantee the right to spend unlimited money influencing elections, influencing candidates, and influencing government representatives. Granted, in Buckley, the Court also wrote:

> "The electorate's increasing dependence on television, radio, and other mass media for news and information has made these expensive modes of communication indispensable instruments of effective political speech."[16]

There it is! That's the justification for changing 200 years of law by the supposed "originalists" on the Court. The Framers had no inkling that the future electorate would become dependent upon television, radio and other mass media for their news. So, although the Framers failed to incorporate words prohibiting Congress from limiting campaign contributions and expenditures, presumably, they would have written the Constitution differently had they anticipated the advent of broadcast media or the internet. In light of the high cost of media access, the Court's decision makes perfect sense — except for two major flaws in the logic. First, "expensive modes of communication" have been "indispensable instruments of effective political speech" since the nation's founding. So it is not new. Second, the electorate has always been dependent upon mass media to learn about candidates, just as politicians have always relied on media to reach and persuade potential voters.

Neither the great expense of campaigning nor the mutual dependence upon media are new phenomena. The Framers were fully aware of both. Nevertheless, they saw no need to prohibit Congress from limiting campaign contributions. They did not prevent legislators from limiting campaign expenditures. Nor did the Framers prohibit Congress from limiting the amount of money people or groups could spend gaining access to our representatives. Furthermore, no previous incarnation of this Court ever found it necessary to equate money with speech in order to impute meaning the Framers never intended.

In truth, candidates for public office need no money at all to speak to the masses. All they have to do is notify reporters where their next rally will be held. If they speak, the media will come. Media are dependent upon candidate speeches to provide news content. This is one of the most important products they sell: information about candidates. Political speeches are the least expensive news to gather and report. They require no investigation, no fact checks, and little editing. So media love to cover candidate speeches. These are the news sources generating the greatest profits.

Still, candidates want as much money as possible for their campaigns. Since they do not need the funding to get their message aired, they must be using it for something else. They use it to win elections, of course, but how? Psychological manipulation. Their money does not go toward sending additional messages, or giving new information, or increasing the quantity of issues discussed. The money gives them the ability to make the same claims over and over again. Almost every candidate now designs some of those messages to suppress their opponents' voter turnout. The more money candidates raise, the more likely they are to win by making their opponents lose.

Money is not speech. From the candidate's point of view, it is winning through manipulation. From the contributors' point of view, it is access. When you and I contribute fifty bucks to a campaign, we do not expect that donation to give us access to the candidate. When AT&T, Bank of America, Pfizer, Exxon, and Dow Chemical collectively contribute more than $5 million to a president's inaugural fund,[17] I'm guessing they expect to be able to get the ear of the president. No corporate employee need ever meet with him. These Robots enjoy so much access to mass media that the views of their management teams are widely understood. They expect legislation favorable to their businesses. They also expect their president to appoint Supreme Court justices to their liking.

This is not meant to be insulting. Your Honors have exhibited ethical behavior beyond reproach, but the Robots got exactly what they paid for. This is a system corrupted by a feedback loop in which money begets laws that enable more money. Here's how that works: Unlimited contributions go to presidential candidates who believe in the good works of corporations. Merely uttering the phrase "free market" provides supposedly unassailable evidence of the need to allow Robots to operate completely free from government oversight. Throughout the past 40 years, presidential candidates who held the wrong beliefs usually failed to get enough money from Robots to run a winning political campaign. Consequently, the winners appointed federal judges and Supreme Court justices who share their beliefs about corporations. Those justices, in turn, twisted themselves into knots to force their decisions to fit with their *originalist* judicial philosophies.

Voila! Money became speech and Robots became people.

Meaning no disrespect or offense, your Honors, but without corporate donations, five of you would not be members of this Court. Yet there you sit. Consequently, we citizens can expect ever-increasing Robot money to overwhelm any and all of our speech. Because, your Honors, money is not speech. It is access. And your decisions have made it nearly impossible for all but one percent of us human beings to gain access to government representatives.

This was not what the Framers envisioned. Obviously, they never anticipated electronic media. However, they also did not know the masses would become dependent upon newspapers for political information. Yet that transformation was complete by the late 1850's.

Publishers in the 18th century had no expectation that most people would buy their *Advertisers*, as many papers were called, because the masses could not afford the three cents! The average wage earned at the time was about 50 cents a day, making the price of a newspaper equivalent to spending $12 today. Imagine spending $12 to get a four-page newspaper! When the Framers embodied free speech in the First Amendment, landowning white men were virtually the only people who could afford a paper. They also were the only people allowed to vote, so publishers tailored their papers accordingly. Two kinds of newspapers were dominant in those early years: One type were mercantile papers that reprinted information about business in England, reported shipping arrivals, and such. The others were political by design, sponsored by a party and often financially supported through government printing contracts.[18] Effective political speech was so expensive, the parties themselves paid for the existence of newspapers. Completely aware of these circumstances, the Framers still chose not to include a single word about campaign contributions in the Constitution, neither directly nor covertly. The original document said nothing about campaign finance.

I must admit, though, truly mass media were unknown to the Framers. Daily papers would not become widespread sources of news until the 1830's when advances in printing and paper-making technologies enabled publishers to sell their newspapers for a penny — the penny papers, they were called.[19] Not only were they cheaper, penny papers typically included three times as much content as their predecessors. Meanwhile, average wages had doubled, effectively cutting the price of a newspaper article by about 96 percent.[20]

Although penny papers were affordable, the new steam presses were expensive. Publishers risked a large amount of capital. Success required a healthy increase in circulation. So content changed to enhance its appeal to the masses. Publishers filled their papers with dramatic news from police stations, criminal courts, and divorce courts. They covered scandals and human interest stories, which helped them establish a loyal readership. They also sensationalized news, reporting made-up "facts" about criminal trials and politicians. Fake news stories were as commonplace in the penny papers as they are today on the internet. Nearly every paper claimed to be the only source of unbiased news. Nationwide, newspaper circulation more than doubled in twelve years, with over 148 million copies selling in 1840.[21]

The most successful newspapers were no longer directly supported by political parties. Instead of sponsoring a newspaper to print favorable editorial content, candidates for public office purchased ads.[22] Fortuitously, even as newspapers were becoming accessible to the middle and working classes for the first time, states were changing laws to allow non-landowners to vote. Penny papers really did become indispensible to this new, much broader electorate in the 1830's and forties.

By 1976, however, when this Court decided money is the equivalent of speech in *Buckley*, the emergence of mass media could only be viewed as a new phenomenon if we were examining history on a geologic timescale. Relative to the duration of United States history, mass media have been around almost since the nation's inception. By pretending otherwise in order to justify reversing an act of Congress, the Court was neither prudent nor *original*. But let's put aside our disagreements regarding whether money is the equivalence of speech, or corporations are equal to people.

Consider the new evidence. Corporations are automatons, Robots that have no choice but to operate outside human moral constraints, legally unable to act for the greater good. Our nation's laws and courts prohibit them from behaving as the Framers believed citizens must behave if democracy is to have any chance of success.

A free people, in order to remain free, must reinstate limits on contributions to campaigns and to political action committees — at least with regard to Robots. Furthermore, We the People should never allow anyone or anything, human or corporation, to speak or contribute money without identifying themselves. Of course, we must be allowed to join groups anonymously. That preserves our right to associate and assemble without fear of reprisal.

Nevertheless, we must always require everyone to identify themselves when they comment in an online newspaper or email. We must be able to identify who or what is lobbying a legislator, running an advertisement, or contributing to a cause or a political action committee. People and Robots make those contributions to influence elections. The rest of us have a right to know who is trying to manipulate us. Instead, we are surrendering to Robots, allowing them to exploit us without limit. We are facilitating nothing less than our cultural suicide.

Your Honors, I humbly rest my case.

From upper left: Timothy McVeigh, Scott Roeder, Paul Jennings Hill, Eric Rudolph, Clayton Lee Waagner, Colonel John Chivington, Philip Klingensmith, Isaac C. Haight, Maj. John H. Higbee, Wade Michael Page, Maj. John D. Lee, Dylann Roof.

4

Conversation with Americans Regarding Terrorism

ADICAL AMERICAN TERRORISTS threaten to crush the culture they claim to defend. Did your stomach twist into a tight knot when you read those words: *Radical American Terrorists*? Let me be clear; I would never advocate labeling anyone that way. I abhor the idea of connecting innocent aspirations of ordinary Americans to views and goals of terrorists. Doing so would marginalize people numbering in the hundreds of millions. People around the world would hate U.S. citizens. We would be enabling a tiny minority to co-opt the adjective "American" to justify hate-filled activities rejecting the culture established by our nation's Founders. So in order to re-establish a more perfect union and ensure domestic tranquility as well as provide for the common defense, I choose to reject using those words to describe anyone, no matter their crimes. But make no mistake, Radical American Terrorists exist.

They have assassinated, bombed, mass murdered, and lynched while proclaiming their notion of red, white, and blue to be the only acceptable view of America. One trait common to their visions is the wish to withhold Constitutionally guaranteed protections and rights from people representing a wide variety of cultural groups. Today's Radical American Terrorists single out one group in particular for exclusion and condemnation: Muslims.

Across the political spectrum, from liberal comedian and talk show host Bill Maher to the newly minted so-called conservative president, people claiming to represent American culture insist on using another label: Radical Islamic Terrorists. They claim this moniker is the most accurate way to describe murderers such as the people who executed the nine-eleven attack, the San Bernardino massacre, and the Orlando nightclub killing spree. Maher and his *Real Time* guest, neuroscientist Sam Harris, claim Islamic culture is the primary driving force behind the majority of extremist acts. In his book, The End of Faith, Harris criticizes humanity's willingness to favor religious faith over reason, regardless of whether the believers are extremists or so-called Moderates.[1]

Many supposedly moderate Muslims support Sharia, which is a set of laws derived from the Qur'an and other religious texts. According to Harris, Moderates together with radical jihadis support killing apostates, former Muslims who have rejected Islamic faith. The two groups comprise 22% of the Muslim population in Britain and 90% in Egypt, Harris said.[2]

"Just say 'Islamic terrorism!'" Maher implored Hillary Clinton, although she was not present on the set of his show in May of 2016. "Just say those words and you'll win the election. Avoid those words and you're going to lose the election." While his words now seem prophetic, I admire Hillary Clinton for persisting in embracing her principles.

Refusal to say Radical Islamic Terrorists, Harris and Maher warn, dooms civilization to fail at defending against attacks and defeating terrorist ideology. Apparently, Islam is the worst religious or cultural ideology on our planet. Too many Muslims, they say, violate women's rights and human rights.

Al Novstrup seems to agree. Novstrup, a Republican representing South Dakota House District 3, believes the government of Dearborn, Michigan has already abandoned the U.S. Constitution in favor of Sharia.[3] Novstrup is so sure he is right that he laughed at This American Life reporter Zoe Chace when she told him she did not believe Sharia law was being enforced by any government within the United States.

"You don't think there's Sharia any place in the United States?" Novstrup asked. "You don't think — wow! Okay. You don't think there's Sharia? I'm just blown away. We're living on two different planets."[4] Yes, Zoe Chace is living on Earth while Al Novstrup resides on Planet Faux News. The claim about Dearborn and Sharia is a lie, which was spread, in part, by National Report, a self-acknowledged fake news site.[5] Nevertheless, elected politicians all over the country have embraced that lie.

While Harris does not claim Sharia is taking the nation by storm, he persists in espousing his own prejudice. "Islam," he said, "is the mother load of bad ideas."[6] In truth, the beauty or ugliness of any religion depends upon the actions of its followers. The foundational texts of Islam, Christianity, and Judaism are filled with admirable mandates for moral conduct, but if taken literally, they also contain a host of contradictions. The Qur'an and Old Testament leave little room for many of the observed facts of our universe. A literal reading of the Old Testament requires us to date the earth at about 6,000 years old. We must reject nearly everything we understand about health, modern medicine, and biology, knowledge that relies on a fundamental understanding of natural selection and genetics. In short, the Bible refutes evolution. Both texts charge their pious adherents to avoid killing, then cite multiple circumstances under which putting someone to death is justified or even required.

In spite of the contradictions and despite many atrocities committed in the name of virtually every religion and nationality, Maher and Harris argue Islam is the worst ideology. Of course, they are careful to say they are not racist or bigoted against Muslims. If a hierarchy of labels were useful, we could label Harris and Maher as Moderate Americans in the same vein that they characterize some adherents to Islam as Moderate Muslims.

Moderates such as Harris, Maher, the new president, and Americans everywhere do next to nothing to stop Radical American Terrorists — although I emphasize again, we should not be using that label. In fact, they take less action than Moderate Muslims do. When Nazis co-opt wide swaths of Idaho, Montana and beyond, we close our eyes.[7] When the Bundy family leads a hostile takeover of a national wildlife refuge in Washington State, the Moderate jury acquits them. When liberals post reminders on my Facebook timeline that Timothy James McVeigh murdered 168 people to enforce his views of America, Moderate apologists post unceasing comments about how his action was an isolated incident, not a trend.

The numbers tell a different story. Far more people have been murdered in the United States by Radical American Terrorists than by all other terrorists combined, including the 1941 attack on Pearl Harbor and the September 11, 2001 attacks in New York, Washington, D.C. and Pennsylvania, but Americans refuse to see it. Even if we consider only those attacks perpetrated after nine-eleven, attacks at the hands of Radical American Terrorists exceed those committed by foreigners and Muslim-Americans on American soil. Again, most Americans refuse to believe.[8]

Many Muslims, on the other hand, do see the harm terrorists are doing to the world. They acknowledge the problem and are committed to helping find solutions. Muslim government leaders in Jordan, Turkey, Libya, Egypt, Saudi Arabia, and Pakistan have contributed money, weapons, and military personnel to fight terrorists in the Middle East.[9] Muslims in America have helped the police and the Federal Bureau of Investigations by providing translation services, tip-offs regarding dangerous plots, and access to mosques.[10] Millions of Muslims throughout the world are trying to thwart disinformation campaigns with their own messages of peace, tolerance, and mutual respect.[11]

Meanwhile, the new president's administration has removed white supremacist and Nazi groups from terror watch lists![12] That reflects some serious denial. Frankly, many of us feel terrorized for the first time since nine-eleven, a terror inflicted by the president, not by Muslims.

❧

We feel powerless. We get continual news reports about how the gap between Republicans and liberals keeps widening. People who identify with either culture increasingly refuse to engage — in conversations, let alone marriage — with members of the other group.[13] But how can we blame liberals for backing away from Republicans? Many Republicans refuse to acknowledge any bigotry in their ranks. They deny racism infuses their policies, and they get angry when anyone points out their apparent prejudices and contradictions.

Yet polls show they support the president's attempt to prevent people from Yemen, Afghanistan, Iran, Sudan, Somalia, Iraq and Syria from entering the United States,[14] despite the body of evidence screaming that zero people, zero, have ever been murdered in the United States by people originating from any of those countries.[15] They support building a wall on the border with Mexico even though fewer undocumented Mexicans live in the United States in 2017 than did in 2008.[16] They insist we are losing jobs to Mexico because of the North American Free Trade Agreement, but simultaneously insist that Mexicans, unable to get good jobs in Mexico, are illegally crossing the border in droves and taking jobs from American citizens. These stories cannot both be true.

Republicans have demonstrated a clear preference for blaming Muslims and Mexicans for the woes of our country when we ought to be devoting our efforts to discovering real causes. Perhaps we should ask ourselves whether supporting our new president is the equivalent of hating Muslims or Mexicans. We also should wonder whether lending our support gives tacit approval to disrespect for women, distrust of U.S. federal court judges, and hatred of journalists.

The new president seems to be making hatred the official foreign and domestic policy of the United States. Moderate American support for all decrees of institutionalized hatred will surely fuel anti-American fire among friends as well as enemies. Furthermore, Republican support for the new policies is encouraging white supremacists to commit acts of violence throughout our country and, apparently, even in Canada.[17] As we relegate Women, Muslims, Latinos, African Americans, and members of the LGBTQ community to the margins of our society, some will certainly rebel. Some will march, as did over three million people on January 21, 2017.[18] Others will rally, as did tens of thousands at airports across the country in the days following the president's issuance of the Executive Order that supposedly was not a Muslim ban.[19] Courts disagreed with the president, finding, among other Constitutional flaws, that it is a Muslim ban.[20]

If we continue to relegate anyone we label as "them" to the margins of our society, we should expect more attacks by people like Micah Johnson, who murdered five Dallas police officers and wounded seven others because he "was upset about the recent police shootings." Apparently, he referred to the shootings of Laquan McDonald, Michael Brown and Walter Scott by police in Chicago, Ferguson, Missouri, and North Charleston, South Carolina. Johnson "said he wanted to kill white people, especially white officers."[21]

Meanwhile, we should be trying to figure out why people are being radicalized when many of us fail to understand how they can feel underprivileged. We ought to be trying to comprehend how and why Dylann Roof became a Radical American Terrorist. "I hate with a passion the whole idea of the suburbs." Roof posted on his website.

"To me it represents nothing but scared White people running. Running ... to escape Niggers and other minorities."[22] He wrote those words June 17, 2015, minutes before praying for an hour with church members at Emanuel A.M.E, then assassinating nine of them. He also wrote that he hated "the sight of the American flag... Many veterans believe we owe them something for 'protecting our way of life.'... But (I'm) not sure what way of life they are talking about. How about we protect the White race and stop fighting for the jews (sic). I will say this though, I myself would have rather lived in 1940's American (sic) than Nazi Germany..." Roof's radicalization began when he Googled "black on white crime." His search led him to a website with hundreds of examples, many of them bogus or misrepresented, of African Americans murdering white people. His radicalization took place solely online, entirely in isolation.[23]

If Roof's hatred and murders were an isolated incident, most of us could be content with locking him in prison, giving him our pity before executing him, then trying to forget his senseless act. Unfortunately, similar sentiments have long motivated a multitude of Radical American Terrorists. "Damn any man who sympathizes with Indians!" shouted Colonel John Chivington as he urged the Colorado Cavalry to massacre defenseless women, children, and elderly Native Americans at Sand Creek in 1864. Think about his words: "Damn any man..." For Chivington, murder was insufficient. To be true men of God, and presumably true Americans, his troops must not only massacre, but also lack compassion for their Cheyenne and Arapaho victims. "It is right and honorable to use any means under God's heaven to kill Indians. Kill and scalp all, big and little." By most accounts, they murdered at least 133 human beings, mostly women and children.[24]

In 1865, a Congressional committee concluded Chivington was the man responsible for the relocation of Cheyenne Chief Black Kettle and his people to Sand Creek, guaranteeing them security. Then, taking advantage of their trust and confidence, Chivington and his troops murdered them, mutilated their bodies, cut out the victims' fetuses and genitalia, and displayed them as trophies in saloons and in a theater in Denver.[25] Such terrorists not only still exist, but we ignore how intricately they are woven into our culture.

⚬⚬⚬

Before Timothy James McVeigh bombed the Alfred P. Murrah Federal Building in Oklahoma City in 1995, before murdering 168 people, he wrote to a childhood friend professing to be inspired by the Declaration of Independence. He finished the 23-page letter with this farewell: "I have sworn to uphold and defend the Constitution against all enemies, foreign and domestic and I will. And I will because not only did I swear to, but I believe in what it stands for in every bit of my heart, soul and being.... I have come to peace with myself, my God and my cause. Blood will flow in the streets, Steve. Good vs. Evil. Free Men vs. Socialist Wannabe Slaves. Pray it is not your blood, my friend."[26] McVeigh's radicalization had begun with a deep fascination for firearms and his conviction that the federal government was violating gun ownership rights guaranteed by the Second Amendment to the Constitution.[27]

People in the Southern States during the Confederate Rebellion were equally convinced their rights had been violated by the federal government — by the temerity American citizens displayed in electing President Abraham Lincoln. Historians note one particular irony of the Confederate Rebellion: States seceded from the Union to avoid losing the right to own slaves, yet Lincoln had no intention of abolishing slavery. Southerners had relied on fake news spread by virtually every newspaper in every Southern state. In speech after speech during the presidential campaign and immediately following his election victory, Lincoln had stated he did not believe the President or Congress had the right or Constitutional authority to abolish Slavery.[28] Nevertheless, the newspapers printed articles filled with lies, bemoaning Lincoln's supposed intent to dismantle legal protections for the practice of owning slaves in the South.[29] Eleven Southern states rebelled, and 620,000 Americans died fighting the Civil War.[30] When John Wilkes Booth assassinated Lincoln in 1865, Booth apparently believed himself to be a patriot, shouting "Sic semper tyrannis! (Ever thus to tyrants!) The South is avenged."[31]

Nearly a century later, police and firefighters apparently believed they were patriots when they battered black children in Birmingham, Alabama. In April of 1963, Martin Luther King, Jr. had been jailed in Alabama for his part in nonviolent protests aimed at ending racial segregation in Birmingham businesses. Three weeks after King's arrest, Southern Christian Leadership Conference organizer James Bevel used a new tactic: child protesters. On May 2, 1963, more than a thousand African-American children skipped school, marched downtown, and entered whites-only stores while singing freedom songs and hymns. Police arrested over 600 of them, some only eight years old. By the end of that day, more than 1,200 protesters crowded into a Birmingham jail that had been designed to accommodate 900 people.

Police had no place to jail more protesters, so when demonstrations resumed the following day, television networks broadcast images of police clubbing children, and firefighters blasting children with high-pressure water, rolling them over and over in the street. People were outraged. World-wide condemnation brought the change King had prayed for. Within one week, he and Fred Shuttlesworth, a local protest organizer, announced an agreement with the city. They would desegregate lunch counters, restrooms, drinking fountains, and department store fitting rooms. Stores would hire blacks as salespeople and clerks. The Birmingham Campaign marked one win for the cause of civil rights.

Another win came the following month, on June 11, 1963, when President John F. Kennedy spoke on national television and radio. He implored Congress and citizens of the United States to support a bill that would grant African Americans equal access to economic and educational opportunities everywhere in the country.

A few hours after that speech, Byron De La Beckwith assassinated Civil Rights activist Medgar Evers, a field secretary for the National Association for the Advancement of Colored People in Mississippi. Evers, following the 1954 Supreme Court decision in *Brown v. The Board of Education of Topeka* [Kansas], had worked to help African Americans gain admission to the University of Mississippi. He also worked to integrate other public facilities, to register African Americans to vote, and to expand their economic opportunities. Beckwith, a member of the White Citizens' Council that had been formed to resist integration, apparently saw himself as a true American while pretending Evers was nothing more than a "chicken-stealing dog."[32] So on June 12, 1963, while Evers attended a late-night meeting with NAACP lawyers, Beckwith hid behind bushes across the street from the Evers home. Evers drove up, turned into his driveway, and parked. As he emerged from his car, Beckwith emerged from the bushes and shot Evers in the back. The bullet ripped through his heart.[33]

Three months after the assassination of Medgar Evers, on September 15, 1963, Ku Klux Klan members bombed a church in Birmingham, killing four African-American girls — Carol Denise McNair, age 11, and Addie Mae Collins, Cynthia Wesley, and Carole Robertson, all age 14.[34]

None of those four little girls, nor Medgar Evers, nor John F. Kennedy lived to see enactment of the Civil Rights Act. Martin Luther King, Jr. did live long enough. President Lyndon Johnson signed the Act into law June 2, 1964. That December, King was awarded the Nobel Peace Prize for his part in bringing worldwide attention to the plight of African Americans and for constantly challenging long-entrenched powers through nonviolent means.[35] Even with passage of the Civil Rights Act, in 1965 few African Americans in the South were registered to vote. For example, only two percent of eligible African Americans were registered to vote in Selma, Alabama.[36]

King met with President Johnson in early February, 1965 to plead the case for voting rights legislation. Shortly afterward, King organized a march from Selma to the Alabama state capitol in Montgomery, 54 miles away. Police violently thwarted the protesters on March 7 and again on the 9th, prompting President Johnson to use national television to pledge his support for the marchers and publicly ask Congress to support the new voting rights legislation. So on the third attempt, March 21st through the 24th, more than 2,000 people successfully marched from Selma to Montgomery. President Johnson signed the Voting Rights Act into law on August 6, 1965,[37] scoring another win for civil rights.

Three years later, James Earl Ray assassinated Martin Luther King, Jr. His death is among the most well known, but just one example in a long list of violence against African Americans. Between 1877 and 1950, white mobs lynched at least 3,959 African Americans, though most historians insist there must have been far more. The number comes from newspaper accounts, but many were never reported or were not reported as lynchings. Consequently, many were never counted.[38] Lynching — using accusation of a crime as justification for murdering the accused — is a thinly veiled tactic used by whites to terrorize blacks and maintain white supremacy.[39]

Sixteen years after King's assassination, white supremacists turned their hatred against American Jews and the institution of a free press. Both campaigns began with a single murder, that of talk show host Alan Berg in Denver, Colorado. Members of The Order targeted him for expressing liberal views on his show. According to the testimony of a founding member of The Order, Berg also "was mainly thought to be anti-white and he was Jewish."[40] So when Berg pulled his black Volkswagen beetle into his driveway, parked, and stepped out, a member of The Order pummeled his body with 12 bullets.[41]

༺ঌo๑༻

While more than a century separates their acts, these assassins shared a strategy: Strike fear in the enemy. Their targets — President Lincoln, African Americans, Latinos, Jews and members of the free press — shared one characteristic: To their assassins, they represented equal rights for non-whites or non-Christians. But no matter how many assassins plague our nation, nor how many victims they claim, we rightly refuse to name them Radical American Terrorists.

Nevertheless, we are mistaken when we disavow any connections between their various acts of violence. Racial animosity permeates America's ethos. Throughout our history we have embraced myths enabling us to commit a host of atrocities. The first and most obvious myth was that our new country would embrace the ideal that "all Men are created equal," and are entitled to "Life, Liberty and the Pursuit of Happiness." Although the Declaration of Independence assured Great Britain's King George III that such rights were given to men by their Creator, apparently slaves were not so endowed. In the first decade after Thomas Jefferson wrote those noble words, the Confederate government made no attempt to offer liberty to slaves.

In 1787, when the Framers decided the Articles of Confederation could not successfully serve the nation's needs, they enshrined slavery in the new Constitution. Article I, Section 2, Clause 3 codifies the counting of each slave as only three-fifths of a human. Article I, Section 9, Clause 1 legally sanctioned the practice of importing slaves until 1808. Article IV, Section 2, paragraph 3 required free states to return escaped slaves to their owners. Finally, Article V, while admirably providing Congress with the ability to propose amendments to the Constitution, expressly prohibited any amendments with regard to slavery prior to 1808. The Framers enacted all that inequality without a single use of the word *slave, slavery*, or any derivation of those words.[42]

Another myth we embrace is called Manifest Destiny, which served as justification for the nearly complete genocide of Native Americans. One of this century's biggest lies, one honored by many Republicans and liberals alike, is that the Constitution enshrines Christian ethics. They ignore the first two clauses of the First Amendment: "Congress shall make no law respecting an establishment of religion, or prohibiting the free exercise thereof..." They also ignore the third paragraph of Article VI, which states, "...no religious Test shall ever be required as a Qualification" to hold any government office in the United States. Many also ignore the rest of the First Amendment, which guarantees the rights to peaceably assemble and to petition the Government.[43]

৵৹৵

Willful ignorance of protections guaranteed in the First Amendment enables the Republican Party and many of its decent Christian supporters to commit themselves to the cause of nullifying women's rights. They work hard to deny women equal pay and to deny them access to reproductive health care. They have waged a political war against a woman's right to choose abortion, to access birth control, and to receive any health care from Planned Parenthood clinics. They wage this war, not to serve their country, not to serve their fellow citizens, but to impose their religious beliefs on the rest of us. And they declare, apparently without guile, that they seek only to enforce the will of the Framers of the Constitution who embodied Christian ethics into American law. Truth, facts, and the words of the Constitution itself be damned, they insist the Framers and the Founders intended this to be a Christian nation.[44] Well, Thomas Jefferson had no such intention. He supported religious free-dom, saying it "does me no injury for my neighbor to believe in twenty gods or no God. It neither picks my pocket nor breaks my leg."[45]

Nevertheless, during the past several years, Republicans who con-trol many state legislatures have passed dozens of laws restricting access to abortion and birth control. Meanwhile, Radical American Terrorists — though we should not call them that — have murdered 11 abortion workers and wounded dozens of others.[46] They have bombed 42 clinics and offices of doctors who provide abortion. They set fire to 182 such clinics[47] and one was set ablaze twice.[48] In short, they have waged a concerted campaign to terrorize doctors and women throughout the country. Moderate Republicans and decent Republican-supporting Christians enable that terrorism by refusing to denounce it strongly enough, and declining to acknowledge how their own protests create an atmosphere in which such terrorist acts are conceived and nurtured. In short, as long as Moderates continue to take little notice of murders committed in the name of American Christianity, the terrorism will continue.

When those Moderate Republicans and decent Christians protest outside abortion clinics, we liberals shake our heads and wonder why anybody in the 21st Century is still anti-women. By framing the ques-tion in those terms, we judge unfairly. Those protesters are not anti-women; they are pro-Christian, or their interpretation of Christianity.

Likewise, when more than three million of us liberals protested the inauguration of the 45th President of the United States, decent Republicans and good Christians all over the country shook their heads and wondered why we were anti-American. They were equally wrong to come to that conclusion. We are pro-American. We are for the America that guarantees equal opportunity to everyone regardless of gender, race, color, religion, or gender identity. We also support the America that guarantees equal access to opportunities for all law-abiding people regardless of their wealth.

We will continue to protest until the 45th President and the Republican party take action to protect women's rights, LGBTQ rights, and the rights of African Americans, Latino Americans, Asian Americans, and children's rights to receive health care and an equal education. Furthermore, we will continue to protest until the Republican party finally releases the most precious hostage of all: Earth.

While we reside on this beautiful planet, the Moderate American organization known as the Republican party, together with its president, hold every living organism in the palms of their hands. In willful ignorance of science, evidence, and facts, they threaten to crush every bit of it. So we march.

We will continue to march, rally, protest, and petition our representatives — even though my state's Republican senator, Cory Gardner, belittles our right to petition. Lately, he refuses to answer his phones or even provide staff to answer them. He does not respond to mail of any kind, and he accuses his constituents of being paid agitators.

Senator Gardner does not act alone. Many Republicans simply ignore sections of the Constitution they find to be inconvenient. Just like Roof and McVeigh, they skip the First Amendment and embrace only the Second. Furthermore, no matter how many times the Supreme Court rules that regulation of firearms is not forbidden by the Second Amendment,[49] they insist their interpretation is right and the Supreme Court is filled with activist justices legislating from the bench. So Republicans turn their heads and ignore how their actions further the cause of Radical American Terrorists.

But they did pay attention when they finally got one of their biggest wishes — They elected a president who said, in his inaugural speech, the magic words they have been waiting fifteen years to hear: "Radical Islamic Terrorists!" Our top military brass, CIA, FBI, and State Department officials all agree: the phrase will serve no purpose except to help ISIL recruit more soldiers for its terrorist army — soldiers in Iraq, in Syria, and perhaps in the United States too. The president also repeated a bad idea originally announced during his campaign: that we should take Iraq's oil. We have 5,000 soldiers working beside Iraqi troops every day. Meanwhile, the new president terrorizes our own soldiers. He publically suggests, so that all Iraqis can hear, that our troops might be there to commit war crimes by stealing their oil. Meanwhile, our soldiers walk side-by-side with gun-toting Iraqis.

We liberals are hoping the Republican party and its champion, the president, will soon decide they are willing to live within the bounds of international law. We hope they can support all the laws of our land, including the ones that protect religious freedom and civil rights. Until then, Republicans and liberals alike must continue to bear the guilt and responsibility for terrorism committed in our names, under the guise of making America great again.

If hearing terrorism associated with that campaign slogan makes you cringe, if you seethe every time you think about that opening phrase: Radical American Terrorist, if even now you are wondering how you can reach the author of such a trashy idea so you can scream at him, if you are wondering how to troll him on Twitter or Facebook or Instagram, please know this: He agrees with you. It is repugnant. It made you more likely to hate him. The phrase made you more likely to hate anyone with similar views. It may even have made you more likely to join some fringe hate group such as the White Knights of the Ku Klux Klan, the Christian Action Network, Atlas Shrugs, Jihad Watch, ACT! for America, Committee for Open Debate on the Holocaust, American Border Patrol, ProEnglish, American Family Association, League of the South...

The list of hate groups goes on and on and on. But remember this: That other phrase, the phrase Republican President George W. Bush implored us not to use, the phrase Barack Obama refused to use — Radical Islamic Terrorism — has finally been spoken, elevated, by an American president. Its regular use is sure to strike fear into the hearts of all Muslims. It is likely to anger Muslims as much as that similar phrase angered you. It is likely to make you and your family, me and my family, every American family, less safe.

5

Conversation with Bill Maher

ill, like you, I've been trying to pin down reasons people keep voting against their own economic self interest in our country. In particular, I want to know how they could vote for a con artist such as the 45th president. Unfortunately, I have come to a disconcerting conclusion: You, Bill, may be largely responsible for Hillary Clinton's loss in 2016. Obviously, you are not the only factor. Millions of people participated in the election. Voters, for instance, certainly had a part. I had a part, but I failed, so I take responsibility for her loss too. Vladimir Putin, James Comey, less than stellar campaigning by the candidate, each played a role in this unlikely tragedy. But to some extent, I blame you. Let me explain.

You keep insisting leaders in our country must use the label, "Islamic terrorists." You are convinced Islam is somehow a crazier, deadlier, more brutal religion than all the others practiced by humans. You have invited onto your show guest after guest who disagree with you — and several who think you are right. On nearly every episode of *Real Time with Bill Maher*, at some point you and your guests devolve into this recurring argument about whether terrorists need to be called Islamic Terrorists. Here is the problem with your stance: Not only have you risked alienating me on this issue — and by the way, I have been a huge fan of yours for years, an esteem that only grew when you released your documentary, *Religulous* — but you drove many formerly Democratic voters away from, well, voting for Democrats.

So you should be asking yourself, "Was Hillary Clinton's loss of the presidential election worth my on-air insistence on being right?"

Normally, I would say your position is no big a deal. After all, it doesn't really matter who's president, does it? Of course, these are not normal times. Our country just elected a president who was, at best, completely ignorant of all information regarding the United States nuclear arsenal, clueless about Russia (he really did not know Russia had annexed Crimea), and knew next to nothing about China, the North Atlantic Treaty Organization, Israel, Europe, Canada, Mexico, Iran, Syria, Iraq and the rest of the Middle East. We just elected a president who, at best, is still ignorant about all information regarding scientific understanding of the efficacy and risks of vaccinations, knows little about public education, and most important of all, believes global climate change is nothing more than an opportunity for other nations to take advantage of us. Furthermore, he won by overtly appealing to bigotry. Who would do that? Who has ever done that? (I'm just gonna let you answer those questions on your own. You have fun with that.)

It is possible this president simply believes his own rhetoric that he knows, "more than the generals do (about Syria), believe me." If he believes his own hyperbole regarding his half-baked policies, I would say our country is in pretty big trouble. Don't you agree?

The picture might be even uglier. After all, it is possible the 45th president understands the issues far better than you and I have given him credit for. In that case, we must ask ourselves, "Why does he want to turn the country in the direction he proposes?"

Any thinking person really could only come to one or two possible conclusions: The direction he intends to turn is the direction that will personally enrich him most. Or maybe he really is being blackmailed, just like the dossier says. You know the one I mean — the dossier put together by former British MI6 agent Christopher Steele.[1]

Regardless of which personality represents the real Donald John Drumpf — the buffoon, the ordinary guy, the guy being blackmailed, or the nefarious genius — I am certain you and I agree, the United States is in trouble. Here is where we disagree: You blame the Democratic Party, Hillary Clinton, and people who refuse to say, "Islamic Terrorism." I, on the other hand, place the blame squarely on your shoulders, Bill.

Why? Well, you have power. You have your own show, so you are influential. In 2016, an average of about 4.3 million people watched each episode of *Real Time*. Admittedly, far more people listen to Rush Limbaugh each week. He has over 13 million regulars. But in 2016, you wielded far more power than Limbaugh did. After all, he never said anything during campaign season that surprised any of his listeners. Not one of the 13 million self-respecting Dittoheads — as Limbaugh's listeners call themselves — none would have been caught dead voting for Hillary Clinton or any other Democrat. But imagine for a moment that Rush Limbaugh had gotten on the air one day in July of 2016 and started his program this way:

Listeners, he did it again. The Republican nominee confounded Democrats, which is not surprising. But he also befuddled establishment Republicans. He confused the mainstream media. And to be honest with you, folks, he's got me dumbfounded too! He likes Vladimir Putin. He's acting like the man's his boyfriend. And he likes Russia's policies toward Syria. They're making the ISIS situation worse, not better, but he likes 'em. And he doesn't understand why we have nukes if we don't use 'em. For the first time in my life, listeners, I'm voting for a Democrat. I know, I know what you're thinking, and you're right: The Democrats couldn't possibly have put up a worse candidate than Hillary Clinton. But I have to vote for her. If I vote for this clown, I think I'll be holding myself responsible for the end of humanity when it comes.

So Bill, first of all, stop laughing. Second, if Limbaugh had ever uttered such a passage, he might have lost listeners or he might have gained some. Okay, he certainly would have lost some. But he might have gained a few Democrats and independents that had never listened to him before. I don't pretend to know how it would shake out. But I am confident he would have swayed the votes of some of his listeners. They love him. Some would have voted for Hillary Clinton, enough that she would have won. He has the listeners and enough influence to have swayed a statistically significant number of voters. Hillary would have won the election. If only Rush Limbaugh were so — what is the word I want? — sane.

Now you should get why I blame you for the Republican's win.

Still don't see it? Then let's continue this imaginary conversation. All right, all right, it's a monolog not a dialog. Anyway, you spent the past year of *Real Time* episodes insisting Democratic leaders were wrong about not using the term Islamic Terrorists. Did you sway any of the leadership? Wait! I know this one! Let me answer: NO!

Not one Democratic candidate for president in 2016 was persuaded by your arguments — not Bernie Sanders the socialist, nor Hillary Clinton the pragmatist; not Maryland's smooth-talking former governor Martin O'Malley, nor Lincoln Chafee who voted to repeal Glass-Steagall because "My dad had died," nor Lawrence Lessig the fake candidate but real Harvard Law School professor. You even failed to persuade former Virginia Senator Jim Webb, and the guy was a Republican until 2006. None of them decided to start using the term Islamic Terrorists just because Bill Maher thinks this is an extremely important label, or because you repeat it on your show every week.

Nevertheless, I feel quite certain — though I have no access to polling data, nor money to commission a poll for proof — some of your viewers were persuaded by your arguments. You never persuaded me, but I'll save my arguments about the label *Islamic Terrorists* for later, if you don't mind. Actually, I don't even care if you mind. You have your show. This is my book. Anyway, some of your viewers must have decided you were right. Some must have thought, "Hey, Bill's right. We should be calling these M****r F*****s Islamic Terrorists!"

The logical consequence, with such wild thoughts tumbling around in your viewers' minds, is some decided they were at odds with all the Democratic candidates for president. Continuing this thread, some found themselves at odds with Hillary Clinton, but voted for her anyway. After all, they were watching your show. They have a lot more in common with Clinton's goals than with Republican ideas. But some of your viewers are freaked out about terrorism. They shouldn't be so frightened, or even concerned about terrorism, but that is another argument I'll save for later. So these people are freaked out. In fact, terrorism has become the number one obsession for them. Where do they go? What will they do? How should they vote?

They voted Republican.

And you caused this. You created their dilemma. Mathematically, this is how it might have worked: Assume about one in eight of your viewers decided they could not vote for Hillary Clinton because she refused to use the label *Islamic Terrorists*. The consequence in Wisconsin, one of the three states that turned the election, was that your viewers swung the election toward the Republican. He won Wisconsin by 22,748 votes. With your influence, one in eight of your viewers voted for him who otherwise would have voted for Hillary. After all, the Republican nominee had "a plan to defeat ISIS immediately, believe me." (By the way, when I re-read that quote, I hear your voice doing his voice. I cannot thank you enough for the comic relief.) Under this scenario, 11,631 former Democratic voters chose the Republican. That amounts to a loss for her and a gain for him totaling

23,261 votes, enough to take the win away from Clinton. Reverse those votes and she wins Wisconsin by 513.

The statistical breakdowns and hypothetical reversals in Michigan and Pennsylvania are more dramatic. In those states, Clinton lost by narrower margins. Again, assuming one in eight of your viewers had not flipped allegiance, Pennsylvania would have favored Clinton by nearly 5,000 votes. She would have won Michigan by over 27,000 votes. Did that really happen? I don't know.

Might it have happened? Probably not. The ratio of viewers who you flipped was likely closer to one in 50, not one in eight, so don't feel too bad. Seriously though, you must have realized by now, some of your viewers made this switch. You unintentionally influenced some quantity of people to flip their votes. Although the election is over and blame is no longer relevant, your show will still have influence going forward. So now I want to turn to the issue of whether the term Islamic Terrorism actually matters, you know, in a safety sort of way. Is the Democratic leadership's refusal to accept this label making citizens and other residents of the United States less safe? Well, how would using the phrase Islamic Terrorism make us safer? I believe embracing the term is already adding to our risk rather than decreasing it.

❧

Using a separate but related story, I'll illustrate. On November 27, 2015 Robert Lewis Dear, Jr. shot and killed three people outside a Planned Parenthood clinic in Colorado Springs, Colorado. At his pretrial hearing, Dear shouted, "I am guilty. There's no trial. I'm a warrior for the babies."[2]

Two months earlier, September 16, 2015, Carly Fiorina, during a televised debate, told a whopper of a lie about abortions. She implored everyone, including Hillary Clinton, to watch a video she claimed revealed a Planned Parenthood doctor performing an abortion and receiving money for subsequent tissue donation. "Watch a fully formed fetus on the table, its heart beating, its legs kicking, while someone says, 'We have to keep it alive to harvest its brain.'"[3]

Although I watched the debate on television and heard her speak the words myself, in my imagination I now hear Boris Karloff speaking. Carly or Karloff, either way, the video doesn't exist. Rather, there is a video, but it does not depict the information Fiorina claimed. Nevertheless, even after the lie was exposed and had been generally acknowledged by every major media pundit, several of them, both right and left, lauded her gruesome description as great politics.

Really, great politics? Or was it motivation for Robert Lewis Dear, Jr. to commit a triple killing two months later?

I blame Carly Fiorina for those deaths — a little. Okay, she didn't pull the trigger. She did not ask anyone to go shoot up a Planned Parenthood clinic. She did not ask anyone to shoot up any clinic or doctor who provides abortions. She just created the atmosphere. She added to the culture that says it's okay to terrorize abortion providers. Just in case you do not believe such a culture exists, let me point out a few more crimes, the perpetrators, and their ridiculously light sentences upon conviction.

Michael Bray was convicted in 1985 of two counts of conspiracy and one count of possessing unregistered explosive devices in relation to ten bombings of women's health clinics and offices of liberal advocacy groups. Stop rolling your eyes, Bill. Not all my examples are from thirty years ago. Read on, I promise I'll bring you right up to date. Initially sentenced to ten years in prison, Bray agreed to a plea bargain and served 46 months. He helped bomb ten health clinics and served less than four years. That disturbs me. But you are familiar with Bray. You interviewed him for your movie, *Religulous*.

Self proclaimed "prisoner of Christ" Shelley Shannon shot Dr. George Tiller in both arms outside his abortion clinic in 1993. She was convicted of attempted murder and sentenced to eleven years in prison. While in prison she confessed to setting several fires at abortion clinics on the West Coast, so her sentence was extended. She is set to be released in 2018.

Shannon failed to kill Tiller, but the so-called Army of God got two bites at that apple. Scott Philip Roeder succeeded where Shannon failed, murdering Tiller in 2009. Prosecutors said the killing did not meet the Kansas standard for capital crime, which would have carried a possible death penalty. Cop killers qualify for the death penalty, not Tiller killers. In a telephone call from prison, Roeder confessed to journalists he had shot and killed Tiller, and declared he felt no remorse. He will be eligible for parole in 2035 after serving 25 years.

Clayton Waagner is expected to be in prison until 2046 for carjackings, firearms violations, bank robbery, and sending letters to more than 500 abortion clinics all over the country. Really, sending letters is a crime? Each letter contained white powder that permeated the air recipients were breathing as they read a note claiming the powder was anthrax. Those letters were sent in November, 2001, two months after nine-eleven when most of us were still shaking from the attacks on the Pentagon and the World Trade Center. Waagner was good at his craft too. His white powder was a relatively harmless insecticide agent that caused the chemical test kits to return a false positive for anthrax.

James Charles Kopp murdered abortion provider Dr. Barnett Slepian. Authorities also suspect Kopp was the shooter in at least four other murders committed against abortion providers in the United States and Canada. Although he is serving a mandatory life sentence, two convicted co-conspirators who repeatedly helped him avoid capture as he travelled back and forth across the U.S.-Canadian border were basically slapped on their wrists. They were sentenced to time already served while awaiting trial.

Eric Robert Rudolph murdered two people and injured over 120 more in a series of bombings motivated by his anti-abortion and anti-gay sentiments. He is serving a life sentence. Paul Jennings Hill was convicted of murdering abortion provider Dr. John Britton and

Britton's bodyguard, James Barrett in 1994. Hill was executed September 3, 2003. Finally, someone received an appropriate sentence for double murder and multiple bombings.

I ronically, I oppose the death penalty. As long as capital punishment is legal, however, I want our justice system to impose death sentences on any and all murderers of abortion providers. Then, I would be even more thrilled if our country banished capital punishment before any of the sentences were executed.

Back to my point: None of those terrorists were Muslim. All these hate-filled people are (or were) self-proclaimed Christians. They belong to a group they themselves call the Army of God. But most of them were not found to be legally insane. Most were not legally incompetent. Only Robert Lewis Dear, Jr. enjoys that distinction. And he struck shortly after Carly Fiorina's phony debate rhetoric. Maybe without that extra bit of motivation from the Republican candidate, Dear's three victims would still be alive.

The acts committed by those abortion foes, the hate speech of Republican candidates, and the lack of appropriate sentences for perpetrators has created an atmosphere in the United States, a culture in which abortion-foe terrorists have been enabled, even encouraged.

When the term Islamic Terrorism becomes normalized, the same atmosphere of violence will permeate our culture. In fact, the term is becoming common already, as is violence against innocent Muslims. You saw footage of the reality television star's political rallies throughout 2016. You saw the violence committed against protesters and people of color. You saw how the Republican nominee himself encouraged such violence and even offered to pay legal fees incurred by anyone who took care of his dirty work for him.[4] You are an intelligent, well-read man, so I feel certain you have read reports of increased violence against Muslims throughout the country in the past year, and especially since the November 8th election.[5]

Republican insistence that we use the term Islamic Terrorism is directly responsible for this increase in violence against Muslims. Do I have absolute proof? Hell no. My evidence is circumstantial. For example, the September 11 attacks occurred more than fifteen years ago. Everyone in our country knows what religion the nineteen attackers and their accomplices claimed to embrace. Yet the increase in violence against Muslims is a recent development, a significant uptick in the past year.

We are negligent if we fail to look inward to try to figure out why white Christian people in the United States committed fewer acts of violence against Muslims in each of the years 2002-2014 than in 2015. In that year, the number of violent acts committed against Muslims increased by 62.5% from the previous year, a 146% jump from the average of years 2002 through 2008.[6]

෨෧

George W. Bush, with whom I had less in common than any president in my lifetime until now, demonstrated a bit of wisdom in this regard. On one hand, he implored the American public to direct their anger at Al Qaeda, at the Taliban who protected Al Qaeda, and at any other people who openly declared themselves to be enemies of, and to hate the United States. On the other hand, he also implored us not to direct hatred or anger toward Muslims in general. Not at Islam. George W. Bush can be credited with keeping Muslim Americans safe throughout the past fifteen years. He kept them safe from other Americans.

The rest of the Grand Old Party, and you, Bill, can be credited with removing that protection. In the past year or so, it has become acceptable to bash Muslims, both figuratively and literally.

I know that sounds harsh.

For me to explain my thinking, first, you have to accept this premise: All humans are stubborn. You and I, like every other person who has ever existed, are prone to reject all arguments and evidence that force us to re-think any long-held beliefs. You are familiar with the psychological terms: cognitive dissonance and confirmation bias.

This explains why so many Americans reject the notions of evolution, a universe that is nearly 14 billion years old, and anthropogenic global climate change despite overwhelming evidence of these phenomena. It is the reason so many parents, and you, Bill, reject vaccinations for children despite the scientific evidence proving they are risking their children's lives. They also risk the lives of everyone else's children, but can we get politicians to require vaccinations? Not in a Republican-controlled state. These parents and their Republican accomplices even reject this fact: The scientist who originally put forward the notion of a link between vaccines and autism, Andrew Wakefield, was exposed as having used fake data. He acknowledged the falsifications. He has long since retracted his own hypothesis. Still, people refuse to get their children the vaccinations that may save their lives and the lives of my students.

Did I forget to mention I teach elementary school? So let me pause here to blast the 45th president and all other Republican candidates who deny the scientific evidence and still use the vaccines-cause-autism meme in their campaign rhetoric.

If you can accept the premise that you are predisposed, as is every normal human being, to be defensive about your position, then you can also be wary of your own bias and be a little more open to some new possibilities. If you have done that, I can lay out my argument.

Since 2009, Muslim bashing has been on the rise, dramatically increasing in 2015. In my opinion, that necessarily leads to further marginalization of Muslim Americans. If we make Muslim Americans feel as though they are not accepted in society, some will withdraw further. Some will withdraw to the Internet, to sites where other marginalized

Muslims hang out. In short, some will become radicalized. They will become terrorists.

And let me be perfectly clear. I am talking about Muslim-American citizens becoming terrorists. If the rest of the country keeps bullying them, why should they love the rest of the country? We should, in fact, expect many to become terrorists. After all, that is the direction toward which we keep pushing them.

୧୨୦୦୨୨

Now, let's talk about Christian terrorists. Dylann Roof comes to mind. He is the young white man who prayed with African Americans in the Emanuel African Methodist Episcopal Church in Charleston, South Carolina. Then he shot and killed nine of them. They were not white people. So he shot them. I am sure he thinks of himself as a good Christian man. So should we label him a Christian Terrorist?

I also think of Timothy McVeigh and Terry Nichols. They were good Christian former U.S. Army soldiers. They detonated an improvised explosive device before the U.S. Army had even coined that ridiculous phrase. Improvised Explosive Device. It's a bomb! But importantly, it's a bomb that no death-merchant corporation made any profit from. So we call them improvised explosives. Timothy McVeigh and Terry Nichols put some ammonia fertilizer together with the rest of the necessary components, put it in a rented Ryder truck and detonated it outside the north side of the Alfred P. Murrah Federal Building in Oklahoma City. They murdered at least 168 people. The death toll might have been 169. Investigators were never able to determine the number of deaths for certain because they could not match a missing left leg to any of the other known casualties. The victims were government employees, so McVeigh and Nichols murdered them. Well, most were government employees. Some were civilians. Nineteen were children. Let us not forget the children.

Anyway, the point is, McVeigh and Nichols were Christians. So we have an important responsibility. We must decide on an appropriate label: Christian Terrorists might be good. Or perhaps Army Terrorists would be better. Maybe U.S. Army Terrorists or just U.S. Terrorists. What's the proper way to label these two guys? What label will have the effect of deterring other young people from wanting to follow their examples and commit similar heinous atrocities against fellow human beings? Please make a suggestion. I would love to hear your thinking on this subject.

Consider this: If we did label Roof, McVeigh, and Nichols as Christian Terrorists, we would have to expand the list. The list should include all those people involved either in murders, arsons, or robberies committed in the name of anti-abortion activities: Eric Rudolph, Robert Lewis Dear, Jr., Michael Bray, Paul Jennings Hill, Scott Philip Roeder, James Charles Kopp, Shelley Shannon, and Clayton Waagner.

✆∽✆

What I'm trying to figure out is why you've decided to be more afraid of Muslims than you are of Christians and Jews. Radicals bring danger, regardless of their religious affiliations. I saw *Religulous*. I had so much admiration for you after seeing that movie. My appreciation exists on at least two levels. The obvious element of the movie that made it terrific was humor. You managed to find many ways to poke fun at religious beliefs without invoking or provoking much anger.

All right, plenty of people were angry after seeing your movie. Not me, though. Perhaps the best element of *Religulous* appeared in the last two minutes before the credits rolled. You cast off all the trappings and veils of humor, looked at the camera and simply told the truth as you saw it at the time. Somewhere in there, I think at the very

89

end of that monolog, you brandished the commandment: "Grow up or die." I loved that.

You and I share a similar background. I am an atheist with two Jewish parents. I consider myself to be culturally Jewish. If memory serves, you are an atheist with a Jewish dad who did not practice the religion at all. My parents did practice, but their siblings and parents always complained they were doing it wrong. Sometimes, you just can't do enough to please your parents. I have always thought religion was, at best, silly. Under worse circumstances, it becomes dangerous. At its worst, religion becomes deadly.

Fundamentalist Christians in the United States of America frighten me far more than any Muslim anywhere in the world. The 45th president seems to fundamentally believe, just as though it is his religion, that his people — and I'm not sure anybody really knows who he considers to be his people — deserve more. They deserve more than anyone who is not one of his people. His people might be white, Anglo-Saxon, Christian Americans. Or his people might only include his immediate family. Hell, his people might be just him. When he says "We..." maybe he means *we* in the royal, singular sense.

I am also afraid of Cliven and Ammon Bundy. They frighten me more than any Muslim. The jury that found them and their companions not guilty scare me too. The atmosphere in the United States that enables a jury to exonerate a group of armed people who took control of a national wildlife refuge scares me.

⚜

Should I be scared? Well, when I was canvassing for the Democratic party this October, wearing a *Hillary* shirt, I approached a house in my own community of Evergreen, Colorado. According to the data I had in my hand, the woman of the house was a registered Democrat, 46 years old. Two men were working on a skiff parked on a trailer in the driveway.

"Do I have the right house for (so and so)?" I ask the men.

"Why?" one asks in a belligerent tone. "Who wants to know?"

So I introduce myself by name and mention that I am a neighbor (true), identify myself as a volunteer for the Hillary Clinton campaign, and hold out my hand for a handshake. This is not my first experience. I know the drill. Always remain calm and courteous.

He never offered to return the handshake. Instead, he drops his tools into the skiff, holds both his hands out, palms up at chest height and approaches me rapidly, as though he's pushing me away.

"You're at the wrong house!"

Then his companion chimes in, "Nobody here's interested in Hillary Clinton."

"Get outa here. You're anti-American!" the first one continues, now screaming.

"I'm leaving," I say, "but does (so and so) live here?"

"Yeah, but she's not voting for that c***, Clinton!" He would have been pushing me off the driveway, but I had turned around and was walking away without any physical aid from him. He kept charging me, though, apparently to be sure of my departure.

"I'll trouble you no further," I finished. I had done my job. I crossed that house and name off my list and identified the woman as an opponent, though she may not have been. How do I know? I never got to speak to the woman, just her husband. Who knows? Maybe he's like the main character in the movie, *Sleeping With the Enemy*: the guy who orders every aspect of his wife's life and beats her up when the soup cans aren't properly arranged inside the kitchen cupboard. He expects them to be in alphabetical order with every label facing forward. Maybe my neighbor tells his wife how to vote and stands behind her while she fills out her mail-in ballot at the kitchen table.

While canvassing for the Clinton campaign, I knocked on several hundred doors, met with hundreds of supporters and opponents. Fortunately, I had only three experiences like the one you just read about. All three were men. All three were not the person on my data sheet. The other two were fathers of the women on my list. In two of the three, I never met the person listed in my data. I did meet one of them, though. She was nice. She said she was undecided about her vote. She had supported Bernie Sanders in the Colorado Caucus. I left some voting information and thanked her. About the time I got back into my Prius — of course I drive a Prius — if I could afford a Tesla I would have paid somebody to canvass for me — anyway, I had just buckled myself in when her dad came out his front door and hurriedly walked to my liberal car.

He asked me, belligerently, just like the guy in the previous story, "Can I help you?" I don't know how to make 'Can I help you' sound menacing in print, but the guy's puffing up his chest, standing tall, and clenching both fists.

"Well, not really," but I introduced myself the same way I described earlier, and added, "I was here to see (so and so)."

"How do I know who you are?" he asks. Yep, he's still belligerent. Now you have to picture this. I'm wearing a white shirt sporting two large, powder blue *Hillary* campaign pins. I've got a backpack on my lap that also features a Clinton sticker. I've also got, by sheer coincidence, my local public school identification card on the dashboard of my car, right next to the driver-side window, face up, picture showing. Nevertheless, I open my wallet to my driver's license and show it to him.

"I'm Todd Lederman, see? I'm a volunteer for..." and you know the rest of my spiel.

"I just don't know why some guy comes knocking on my door asking for my daughter. You could be a predator or something." His words say he's being protective of his daughter, but his tone says, "How dare you live in MY community and support Hillary Clinton!"

"As I said, I'm working for the presidential campaign." At this point, I pick up my teacher badge and show it to him. "And by the way, I'm a public school teacher. I've been fingerprinted and investigated. It's a requirement for getting the job."

I had many wonderful experiences while canvassing. I met plenty of people who were cordial, even some who were Republican supporters. But I'm sharing the negative episodes because they scared me. I never felt afraid for my personal safety. This fear is different. I am frightened for a country in which a large segment of the population has concluded that people who disagree with them are evil. Mitt Romney implied as much when he spoke of the 47% — people who are not financially successful, so by definition, they must be lazy and dishonorable. We Americans face real peril when our neighbors decide our support for a candidate they oppose proves we are un-American and unworthy of decent treatment or civil conversation.

I worked hard and long hours with hundreds of volunteers trying to get Hillary Clinton elected. Several of my fellow volunteers gave more time than I was willing to offer because I didn't quit my job teaching. I thought about taking leave from my regular job so I would have more time to work for the campaign. Not seriously, but the idea did occur to me. That is how afraid I was of the Republican Party's nominee.

This was the first time I worked for any political campaign, even though I've always been a junkie for political news and always voted for Democrats. Sometime last May, when it was obvious the Republican nomination was sewn up, I said to myself and to my wife, "If I don't do everything reasonably within my power to make sure this dictator-loving, know-nothing lunatic loses, I will not be able to live with myself next year."

So I volunteered. Having put in less than every second of my time, however, I still feel a little guilty. See what I mean? Culturally Jewish.

Now that I've admitted my guilt, let's have a look at what you could have done differently, Bill. Do you really believe we need to be terrified of terrorists? Statistically, you're dead wrong about this. If we add up all the murders perpetrated by terrorists in the United States, let's see what we get. First, we need a list.

Perpetrator of Terror	Death Count
1859 John Brown (4 victims, 10 perpetrators)	14
1864 Colonel John Chivington, et al, Sand Creek Massacre	133
1864 John Wilkes Booth	1
1881 Charles J. Guiteau	1
1901 Leon Czolgosz	1
1927 Andrew Philip Kehoe	44
1928 Leung Ying	14*
1941 Japan (No war declared, so, terrorism)	2,403
1946 Vincent William Smith	9
1963 Lee Harvey Oswald, (insane, not terrorist)	0
1966 Charles Whitman	18
1973 Mark James Robert Essex	9
1984 James Oliver Huberty	21
1986 Henry Patrick Sherrill, (Gave rise to term Going Postal.)	14
1990 James Edward Pough	11
1991 George Pierre Hennard	23
1999 Mark Orrin Barton	12
1999 Eric Harris and Dylan Klebold	13
2001 Al Qaeda, et al	2,996
2002 John A. Muhammad and Lee Boyd Malvo	11
2003 Jiverly Antares Wong	13
2007 Seung-Hui Cho	32
2009 Malik Nidal Hasan	13
2013 Aaron Alexis	12
2015 Dylann Roof	9
2015 Rizwan Farook and Tashfeen Malik	14
2016 Omar Mateen	49

*Convicted of murdering 11 people. May have killed three others.

G oodness, what a long list! I have not included a name unless the perpetrator killed at least nine people, with some notable exceptions. For example, I included assassins of U.S. Presidents. You probably also will notice the list is missing some people mentioned earlier: Robert Lewis Dear, Jr., for instance. I have tried to leave out massacres committed by people who were found to have been incompetent or insane, rather than politically or religiously motivated. The list, as it exists so far, represents 6,059 lives taken by "terrorist" activities. The murders committed that are not detailed in the above account — those attributable to terrorism but which numbered fewer than nine deaths per incident — amount to another 457 lives taken. Together, that totals 6,516. If we only include the murders since 9/11/2001 — the murders we think we should worry about now that Muslims have been declared the scourge of the Earth, but not including the 168 lives taken by home-grown Christian Terrorists Timothy McVeigh and Terry Nichols — that total comes to 3,606. Please note, I am certain that I included some murders that you would not consider to be acts of terrorism. That actually works in my favor for the argument. It means any probability forecast detailed in the next paragraph actually overstates the likelihood of death by terrorism, while understating the comparisons you will read about in a moment. Read on, you'll see what I mean.

If we take the 3,606 murders perpetrated during a period of a bit over fifteen years and extrapolate throughout the average life span of about 79 years, our president has one chance in 18,000 of being killed by terrorists, regardless of their religious affiliation. My wife is twice as likely to get killed by the accidental discharge of a gun, fired either by herself or someone she knows. For the record, we do not own any guns, but several of our friends and relatives do. One of your guests on your program is 136 times more likely to die in a car wreck. And you, Bill, because you partake of cannabis as you so frequently remind us, assuming you smoke the demon weed, you may be 3,265 times more likely to die of lung cancer than at the hands of terrorists, no matter what religion they profess to embrace. Or maybe not — Some research shows no correlation at all between lung cancer and marijuana use.

Do you really believe we need to slap these people with a label that says DANGER! Islamic Terrorists? While that might make you feel safer, it will not actually make you be any safer. Must you continue to claim that Muslim craziness is somehow worse than Jewish, Christian, or Buddhist craziness? You probably cannot imagine supposedly peace-loving Buddhists being violent. So take a look at Myanmar and check out the violence against the Rohingya, a Muslim ethnic group.

～♉～

Circling back to my main point, I hope you will consider backing off your fear mongering a bit. Fear of the 45th president's administration and what it may bring is completely legitimate. Fear of terrorists, regardless of their religious beliefs, is way overblown in this country.

If we want to prevent further homegrown terrorists in the United States, we should make sure all people, not just white people, get a great education starting when they are three years old. We should make sure everyone has access to decent, affordable health care. We should make sure a parent can take paid family leave for at least three months after their baby is born. We ought to educate people about how parents abusing their children perpetuate a cycle of violence, and how mass murderers from every religious background are almost always people with histories of violence against women.[7] We should make sure every full-time worker, no matter the job, earns a living wage. This means we have to stop fetishizing manufacturing jobs lost to technology and start making sure every job performed by a human pays well. Most of all, we have to make sure all these advantages are openly and completely available to everyone, regardless of their race, creed, color, gender, or religion. In the next chapter, *Conversation with Blue Collar Workers*, read a detailed description about how to solve our economic problems.

6

Conversation with Blue Collar Workers

Blue Collar Workers, you deserve better. You work hard, go home, do dinner, help with homework, and watch a little television. Then you collapse in bed until it's time to wake up and do it all again. At the end of the week you get a paycheck, but it's not big enough. It's not enough for the kind of house you wish you could afford. Your labor pays for a meager roof, food for the family, and the fees your children's public school charges at registration. You might make enough money to take your kids to the amusement park, buy them video games, a bicycle, maybe pay for summer camp. Then again, you might not. And your hard work simply does not bring in enough money to pay for your children to go to college.

Then Vice Presidential Candidate Paul Ryan (R-WI) tells the whole country you're a leech on society. You — because you plan to use your Social Security and Medicare benefits when you retire, or you receive Medicaid, or you get food stamps, or because you receive benefits from Aid to Families with Dependent Children — you're a taker.[1] This might make you angry, but don't be mad at Ryan or Republicans for calling you names. You shouldn't get angry at Mitt Romney for claiming you're worthless in his eyes and useless to the country because, as he claims, you pay no income taxes.[2]

No, the real reason you should be mad at Ryan, Romney, the 45th president, and the whole Republican Party has nothing to do with what they say or how they insult you. You should be furious that they keep enacting laws to make rich people far richer, offer no way for the poor to escape poverty, and depress wages for the Middle Class. That should keep you up nights. You should be angry because they seem to sincerely believe anyone who is not rich must be a taker. If you're not rich, they think you're lazy and simply don't work hard enough or long enough hours.

Of course, you weren't buyin' what Romney and Ryan were sellin'. That's why Barack Obama won his reelection bid in 2012. But in 2016, a new guy comes chuggin' down the track blowin' a new whistle with a new message:

gonna GET you great JOBS. gonna GET you great PAY.
gonna GET terrific HEALTHcare on the VERy first DAY.
EV'ryone will GET it and it's GONna be a KICK.
WINning's gonna BE the only THING to make you SICK.
beLIEVE me!

And Blue Collar Workers, you got on board. You voted for the reality television star who brags about sexually assaulting women. Apparently you like the guy's tough talk against free trade agreements with Mexico and Canada: "NAFTA[3] is the worst trade deal maybe ever signed anywhere."[4] His trade policy might be the only stance he touted during the campaign that he honestly believes in, but he's got it wrong.

The real reason government has not worked for you since January 20, 1981 is, well, think about it. What happened January 20, 1981?

That's right. Ronald Reagan happened. We've raised this guy up like a god. In fact, he hurt our country as no other president has since James Buchanan led the nation toward Civil War. Reagan was responsible for putting the country back on a dangerous path leading toward cruel levels of inequality. At home, he busted unions, put health care costs on an inflationary path, and cut taxes for the wealthy. His administration laid the groundwork for news media that have no accountability to consumers of news and no regard for the greater good of the country. Abroad, his policies inflicted unprecedented damage to our standing in the world. His administration defied Congress, broke the law by selling weapons to Iran to obtain release of hostages in Lebanon and to fund terrorist operations in Nicaragua.

◊

That warrants repeating. Bear with me a bit, then we'll get back to how Ronald Reagan's policies decimated the Middle Class. Meanwhile, let's explore how his administration perpetrated, in essence though not in name, a notorious act of treason. Ronald Reagan's administration wanted to give money to a group of terrorists in Nicaragua called the Contras. They were trying to overthrow a socialist government. Although no one ever accused Reagan of being anti-social, he was definitely anti-socialism, so he supported the Contras. A majority of Congress opposed the Contras, however, because the government they sought to overthrow had been democratically elected. So Congress passed the Boland Amendment, part of the Defense Appropriations Act of 1983, which President Reagan signed. The Boland Amendment prohibited military support for the Contras. Reagan's administration didn't like that. Said we're gonna get those boys some money anyway.[5]

Meanwhile, a group of Iran-backed terrorists in Lebanon called Hezbollah were in the process of kidnapping 104 Europeans and Americans and holding them for ransom. Iran was enmeshed in a brutal war against Iraq, its neighbor to the west. The United States viewed the Islamic Republic of Iran as its enemy because Iranians had held 53 U.S. diplomats hostage from November 4, 1979 until, hmmm, January 20, 1981. What a coincidence! So in 1982, the United States supported Saddam Hussein and Iraq in the war, supplying Iraq with weapons, money, and intelligence gathered from U.S. spy satellites.[6]

We still do not know for sure, but Iran may have been directing Hezbollah to take American hostages in Lebanon. We do know Iran had undeniable influence on the kidnappers. So Reagan's boys made a deal with Israel. And Iran. And the Contras. On behalf of the United States of America, Israel shipped TOW anti-tank missiles and Hawk anti-aircraft missiles to Iran. There it is. That's the treason. After the first two shipments, the United States started dealing with Iran through two private intermediaries: Richard Secord, a retired U.S. Air Force officer; and Albert Hakim, an Iranian-American businessman. Iran paid a marked-up price for the weapons — $12 million extra for more than 2,500 missiles. About $2 million went to the Contras. Presumably, the other $10 million never left Secord's and Hakim's pockets.[7]

In case you think you read that wrong: Yes, our country sold missiles to our enemy, Iran, while also giving money and weapons to Iraq so the two countries could wage war against each other. We used the profit from the missile sales to support a group of terrorists in Nicaragua trying to overthrow their democratically elected government. That was American foreign policy in the 1980's — the Reagan years.

In the 1990's, under George Herbert Walker Bush, we waged our own war against Saddam Hussein and Iraq. We sent our troops to face an army partially equipped with, you guessed it, American-made weapons left over from its war against Iran. We won the war, forced Iraqi troops to evacuate Kuwait, but left Saddam Hussein in place as president-dictator of Iraq. That was American foreign policy from 1989 through 1992 — the Bush 41 years.

With the new millennium, during the George W. Bush presidency, we again waged war against Iraq, this time overthrowing Saddam Hussein after using politicized intelligence to wrongly accuse him of harboring terrorists and manufacturing weapons of mass destruction. That was American foreign policy from 2001 through 2008 — the Bush 43 years.

Today, although the new government in Iraq is an ally, we still consider Iran to be our adversary. We have also added to our enemies list Syria and ISIL, who are at war with each other. ISIL confiscated American-made weapons from Iraqi troops it defeated in 2014, so again, our enemy has our weapons. Turkey is our ally, but in our conflict against ISIL we've enlisted and armed their enemy, the Kurds in Syria and Iraq. In addition to arming, once again, both sides in a proxy war, our soldiers are engaged in a hot war against both sides. We're fighting ISIL with soldiers on the ground while also launching missiles against the Bashar al Assad regime in Syria. And Russia — the country who used cyber warfare to manipulate American public opinion in our 2016 presidential election — Russia has combatants in the same fight.[8] What could possibly go wrong?

***

I ran-Contra and its fallout was not the only legacy Ronald Reagan left us. He deregulated banks, leaving the economy of the entire world continually vulnerable to collapse. In all fairness, one deregulation was signed into law by President Jimmy Carter. But the major overhaul began with Reagan's presidency, and the high regard for deregulation continued because of Reagan's popularity.[9] The Savings and Loan meltdown followed shortly thereafter, in 1986. That was quickly followed by the Industrial bank collapse of 1987. The only surprise about the inevitable financial meltdown of 2007-2008 was how much time elapsed between these crises.

The lesson we should learn is this: Take away all the risks assumed by people running banks and securities brokerage firms, leave in place rewards that can reach billions of dollars for a CEO who takes those risks with other people's money, and collapse must follow. No matter how ethical most bankers may be, without government regulation and oversight, at any given moment there will always be several money manipulators risking our financial security and the smooth functioning of the world's economy for the potential reward of amassing the wealth of kings. From 1866 — one year after the end of the U.S. Civil War — until the Crash of 1929, the United States experienced seven major, nationwide bank crises. That amounts to one collapse every nine years.[10]

After Franklin Delano Roosevelt signed several laws in the 1930's designed to protect depositors and stimulate the economy by allowing people to trust banks again, we had zero financial collapses for the next 56 years. None. The Glass-Steagall provisions of the 1933 Banking Act prevented banks from loaning money for stock market purchases or operating as stock brokerage firms. Those practices had led to the 1929 stock market crash, which in turn led to the collapse of more than 9,000 banks by early 1933.[11] Other sections of the Banking Act created the Federal Deposit Insurance Corporation, which guaranteed depositors would not lose their money if their bank failed. Rampant deregulation, promised and delivered by Ronald Reagan and the presidents who followed him, destroyed a half-century of stability in which American companies could do business safely.[12]

Also under Reagan's administration, the Federal Communications Commission deregulated broadcasting. The FCC stopped enforcing the Fairness Doctrine, unleashing a 30-year barrage of lies from so-called conservative channels. The FCC had established the Fairness Doctrine in 1949 under authority granted in the Communications Act of 1934. It required broadcasters to devote some time to controversial matters of public interest, and to present contrasting views. If a radio station or television network presented any editorial opinion, it had to present opposing views. The broadcaster could lose its license if it failed to honor this concept. The reasoning for the Fairness Doctrine was simple: From the 1930's through the 1970's, available technology limited news transmissions via radio wavelengths to a few dozen stations in any geographic area. Those wavelengths, according to the Communications Act and its predecessor, the Radio Act of 1927, belonged to the people, not to the corporations that used them. So the federal government issued licenses to companies to use specific wavelengths, but only on condition that their news and editorial content served the greater good of the people. In other words, each broadcaster had to present all sides of a controversy.[13]

On several occasions, broadcasters claimed the Fairness Doctrine violated their free speech rights by forcing them to give free airtime to people who wanted to present opposing viewpoints. The courts always decided the Fairness Doctrine itself was not in violation of the First Amendment to the Constitution. "It is the right of the viewers and listeners, not the right of the broadcasters, which is paramount," wrote Justice Byron White in the unanimous 1969 Supreme Court decision in *Red Lion Broadcasting Co., Inc. v. FCC*.

Red Lion had personally attacked journalist Fred J. Cook on air. The FCC ordered Red Lion "to send a transcript of the broadcast to Cook and provide him reply time, whether or not Cook would pay for it." The Court upheld the FCC order, however, in a portion of White's opinion he acknowledged that scarcity of broadcast frequencies had prompted the original Congressional regulation, and that improving technology was enabling more channels.[14] He implied that existence of a lot more channels, if that were possible, might make the Fairness Doctrine unnecessary. If people had many places to hear and watch news, they would have opportunities to be exposed to many points of view without placing the burden for diversity on any single broadcaster.

The 1980's changed everything. Far superior technologies greatly expanded cable capacity. In any given area of the country, the number

105

of television stations grew from a half dozen to several hundred. In 1987, the FCC reasoned that the Fairness Doctrine no longer needed to be enforced.[15] Since then, the Supreme Court has had no occasion to consider its validity. The only reason Fox News Channel can bill itself as 'fair and balanced' is because the FCC chose not to enforce fairness or balance. The FCC decision also enabled the on-air existence of Rush Limbaugh, Glenn Beck, Alex Jones, and other notorious disseminators of faux news. Reagan's administration, in my opinion, gave us the worst set of policies since the years preceding the end of slavery.

$\wp \infty \wp$

George H.W. Bush's presidency proved to be slightly better than Reagan's, although his emissary delivered a miscue that may have encouraged Saddam Hussein to invade Kuwait.[16] With that mistake, we were forced to form an international military coalition to force Iraq to leave Kuwait — the First Gulf War. Bush tried to pay for that war by raising taxes. That was the right thing to do, and it may have put a temporary brake on the widening wealth gap, but it cost him his re-election bid — Ever since Ronald Reagan's presidency, the Republican Party has never seen a tax increase it was willing to embrace. Consequently, Republicans stayed away from voting booths in the 1992 presidential election. Then Bill Clinton, following the failure of Hillary Clinton's healthcare reform proposal, turned the Democratic party so far right it mirrored the Republican party of President Dwight D. Eisenhower's administration. After Bill Clinton, George W. Bush widened the gap further by giving tax breaks to the already super wealthy.

Barack Obama could have made sweeping changes during his first two years, which would have cemented his popularity throughout the rest of his presidency. Unfortunately, the Republican party would not work with the president in good faith. He failed to recognize their complete dedication to obstructing progress until it was too late to become effective. His moment had passed because you guys, you blue-collar white workers, allowed Republicans to take control of the House in 2010.

Lack of progress was not President Obama's fault. The blame does not lie with Hillary Clinton. It lies square in the lap of the Republican Party. Instead of punishing Republicans for fighting against President Obama's progressive agenda, you didn't show up to vote in 2010. You again failed to show up in 2012 and 2014. And when you finally did vote in 2016, you misunderstood the history of the previous six years, in fact, the previous 36 years, and voted for the Republican nominee. Workers, you gotta get over this obsession with thinking black people or Mexicans stole your work, or bad trade deals cost you your job.

I n all likelihood, technology stole your job. Coal jobs, for example: Coal workers, or former coal workers in Ohio, Kentucky, and West Virginia, overwhelmingly voted for the Republican in 2016. Many were mad at Hillary Clinton when she said, candidly, that jobs would continue to disappear. She told them she supported policies to help them get training for other careers, and she specifically suggested careers in clean renewable energy production.[17] The Republican nominee promised to bring back their coal mining jobs. He claimed, "The Obama-Clinton war on coal has cost Michigan over 50,000 jobs."[18] He lied. Bigly.

For starters, Michigan has never been a big coal-producing state. The state had only 7,000 people employed in all mining jobs during the decade leading up to 2016. Nationwide, the number of coal miners peaked in 1923 at 798,000 people. At that peak, those miners were producing almost 700 million tons of coal per year. But coal production peaked 88 years later in 2011. Almost 1.1 billion tons were produced by only 80,000 miners. That's about one-tenth as many people employed, but they mined more coal, 70% more. Those job losses reflect a century of improvements in technology and have nothing to do with environmental policy.

From 2007 to 2008, the number of people employed in the wind power industry leapt from 50,000 to 85,000 and surpassed the number of coal miners for the first time.[19] Again, these wind power jobs had nothing to do with President George W. Bush or his policies. The jobs arrived because the price of producing electricity from wind decreased. As the technology improved, more people and companies wanted wind power, which put more people to work in that industry.

During the same years, the number of people employed by the solar energy industry also soared. In 2006, when the industry itself was not yet keeping tallies on its total employment, industry representatives estimated employment to be about 30,000 people. By 2010, excellent industry-wide records were being tabulated, and total direct employment had reached 93,000. As with wind power, the solar industry surpassed coal in terms of job creation. By the end of 2016, employment in solar had nearly tripled to 260,000.[20] Did that growth occur because President Obama got legislation passed to help the solar industry? No. In spite of many infamous reports about the failure of Obama's policies such as the defaulted loan made to Solyndra, after the 2009 stimulus bill, President Obama was not able to get a single bill passed to help curb anthropogenic global climate change — By the way, that's fancy talk for: "People be cookin' the planet." No, those 209,000 jobs arose because the cost of producing electricity using solar has plummeted. Again, the technology dramatically improved.

Neither solar nor wind energy, however, are responsible for the recent loss of coal mining jobs. Nope. That can be blamed solely on hydraulic fracturing, better known as fracking. Use of this technique together with improvements in horizontal drilling technology led to substantial production increases from each well. The new technologies enable previously low-producing wells to remain in service, and they allow production from shale. In short, the technology allows greater production at less cost, so much so, that the price of natural gas fell from over $14.55 per million Btu (British thermal units) in 2008 to $3.70 in January of 2017. By the way, the price dropped as low as $1.59 in March of 2015, which is lower than the cost of coal — and the reason so many energy companies capped their wells during the following year. Natural gas prices have stayed below $5.32 since July of 2010.[21]

The practical effect of those prices on the coal industry cannot be overstated. Coal-fired electrical power plants cannot easily be converted to use solar or wind energy, but they can and have been converted to use natural gas. For example, in December of 2016, NRG Energy announced it had completed conversion of four coal-fired plants to natural gas. Two plants were in Pennsylvania, and one each in Illinois and Louisiana. The company claims the conversion will reduce carbon emissions in those plants by 80%[22]. In 2016, American Electric converted its Clinch River plant in Virginia from coal to natural gas.[23] Dozens of formerly coal-fired power plants have been converted in the past few years and dozens more are slated for the next few years.[24]

The oil and gas industry's use of fracking is just one example of technology taking employment away from people. But that is not the whole story. Yes, fracking cost 15,000 miners their jobs in 2016. Employment level in coal mines dropped from about 80,000 to 65,000. Meanwhile, the main sources of new power generation in the United States are wind and solar, and they produce jobs. Much of the price of traditional power plants is the fuel. When we buy that fuel, some money goes to people who inherited ownership of underground oil, gas, and mineral rights, but most of the money goes to corporations that extract the fuels. Workers receive little, because machinery performs most of the labor.

On the other hand, sunshine and wind are free. Much of the money we invest in solar and wind energy pays for workers to install power generation equipment. When we consumers pay for solar and wind power, we are paying human labor. We create local jobs. We don't have to choose between low prices or jobs, between protecting our climate or jobs. Solar and wind provides inexpensive power, clean air, and good jobs.

♾

My main point is that technology, not free trade, is a job killer. By the way, I am not arguing against improving technology either. I am simply asking all the people in our country — policy makers, workers regardless of the color of their collars, and voters — to recognize where our problems really originate. Only when we confront the source of our wealth gap can we begin brainstorming solutions that have any chance of succeeding. If we keep spending our time solving nonexistent problems, we will continue to fail. We will stay divided. We will remain vulnerable to politicians, corporations, and the mega wealthy who hold us down by pointing fingers at the Other — other Party, other country, other color, other religion, other gender, or anyone who simply failed to become rich. Our labor force is not suffering because of NAFTA, CAFTA, the WTO[25] or any other free trade scheme. Blue Collar Workers, you're suffering from an acute case of technology.

From 2000 through 2010, productivity growth caused 85% of job losses in the United States. Meanwhile, trade accounted for just 13% of the job losses, but the economy created 15 times as many new jobs as were lost to trade. Let me translate that: 85% of the jobs lost in the country in that decade were lost to robots, computers, and similar technologies. If you lost your job, there is a 7 out of 8 probability you lost it to a technological breakthrough, not to an undocumented worker, nor to some unseen laborer in Mexico, India, Vietnam, or China. Imports from China did displace about 982,000 workers from 2000 through 2007.[26] That is about 10,000 jobs a month. To put that in perspective, our population is growing by about 189,000 people every month. Now consider this: After the recession ended in 2009 — the recession President Obama inherited from President Bush — our economy added 23 million new jobs, but lost 8 million old jobs to trade and technology, resulting in 15 million more workers gaining employment.[27]

Some workers are rightly asking, are they good jobs? The honest answer is, not as good as they could be. If unions were strong and state and federal laws protected union workers' rights, 21st-century jobs could pay you a living wage again. But the place to direct your blame is not at trade, blame is an arrow that should be aimed and fired directly at Governor Scott Walker (R) of Wisconsin, Governor Rick Snyder (R) of Michigan, Governor Rick Scott (R) of Florida, and Governor John Kasich (R) of Ohio who have been staunch supporters of any and all laws limiting the power and ability of unions to collectively bargain for higher wages. You can aim that arrow at Daryl Metcalfe (R), member of the Pennsylvania House of Representatives who has submitted and supported union-busting legislation in his state. He calls his legislative agenda a "right to work" issue, a question of giving Pennsylvanians "...the basic freedom to choose which private organizations they will join or support." That is the lie given to Right to Work laws in exactly half the United States. On his official website, Metcalfe writes: "...Right to Work states consistently lead the nation in all aspects of real economic growth and overall quality of life." Do they? Let's take a look.

In 2015, of the eleven states with the fastest growing economies, five were states with right to work laws. Six were not. Of the ten states with the most rapidly declining economies, six were states with right to work laws. Four were not. Do you see the obvious correlation? Neither do I! There does seem to be a very small correlation — in the direction to refute Metcalfe's assertions.

Oh wait! I left out some important data: population. If we take into account the population of those states, a more obvious result comes into focus. The states that had high economic growth rates and right to work laws have almost 26 million residents, while more than 78 million people live in the states with high economic growth and laws that still protect unions. Metcalf seems to be wrong. Way wrong. He couldn't have lied on purpose, could he?

To be completely fair, we also should look at the population in states with low economic growth: right to work states had 11.9 million people versus 15.6 million people without such laws. So that would seem to lean in Metcalfe's favor. In all honesty, though, no scientist would ever consider this to prove anything one way or the other about the effects of right to work laws. Looking at evidence from many decades, these laws do not seem to have a measurable impact on a state's economy that researchers have been able to isolate.

They do have an impact on business leaders' choices regarding where to locate. In other words, they allow one state to poach businesses from another state. But this poaching comes with a cost: Right to work laws have a dramatic, measurable, downward effect on wages, especially for low- and middle-income laborers. They impact a greater proportion of African Americans, Latino Americans, and young people of all races and ethnicities. So Metcalf's claim of improved "overall quality of life" would seem to be based on something other than wages or purchasing power. These laws are mislabeled. They should be called "Right to Work for Less" laws. Another appropriate name might be: "Right to Further Enrich the Mega-Wealthy," because that is their practical effect. They have, in my opinion, played a large role in the continuing saga of the ever-widening wealth and income gap among citizens of the United States of America since Ronald Reagan's presidency began on January 20, 1981.

So my point is this: Please point your arrow of blame where it belongs — at the Republican Party and Ronald Reagan and all the people who bow down to him and his legacy. His legacy of continual bank industry deregulation may be the reason you lost your job, and his legacy of union busting is the reason you cannot get good wages at your new job.

Furthermore, Reagan's legacy of tax cuts has been a major driver behind the increase in wealth inequality throughout the past three decades. Poor and middle-income people tend to spend most or all of their money, including any windfall they receive from lower taxes. Rich people do not. Rich people already buy whatever they want. Giving them a tax break simply enables them to bank more wealth. But if we raise taxes on the mega-wealthy, that causes them absolutely no harm and no harm to the economy.

The logic is simple: Raise taxes on the mega-wealthy. Tax about 60 percent of their income or gains that exceed $200,000 for a family of four. Such a tax would not cause them to curtail spending. Therefore, their greater tax burden will not reduce employment. My employment is made possible by your spending, while your employment is made possible by my spending. Consumers are the true job creators. If the tax increase does not cause anyone to consume less, the tax increase will not result in job losses.

Tax cuts also are directly connected to our nation's soaring debt. A few tax cuts here and there, a couple unfunded wars, and one Great Recession adds up to a load of debt. Sometime in 2017, U.S. debt exceeded the threshold of $20 trillion. Rewind the clock and remove all the federal government tax cuts since Ronald Reagan's presidency, and the debt would not exist. Workers, we really do need tax reform. We need to increase taxes, especially on the wealthy.

∞

Blue Collar Workers, if you really want to improve your station in life, consider withholding your support for "Aw, shucks" Republicans straining to sound like you. That well-practiced drawl is a con. They get you to vote for them while they rip apart the Middle Class. They systematically destroyed every institution that led to the creation and growth of that Middle Class. They have worked continually to dismantle unions and a fair minimum wage, and that work continues. They have worked to increase taxes on the Poor and Middle classes while decreasing tax on the wealthy, and that work continues. They have reduced availability of free college tuition for military veterans. They constantly diminish the effectiveness of college grant programs for students who have aptitude but lack money. They have reduced public investment in scientific investigation, and they are working to reduce it further. They have decreased investment in road and bridge construction and in energy infrastructure. They want to continue reducing. In short, Republican policies since 1981 have kept poor people poor and strangled much of the Middle Class, leaving them poor too.

Meanwhile, their policies have skyrocketed the mega wealthy into an entirely new class whose income doubled during the decade in which the rest of us experienced the Great Recession. For 80 percent of us, our income decreased during the same decade.

Much of the mega wealthy do not work. They get income from their shares of ownership in corporations. In other words, they earn income and gains on their capital. In addition, they pay lower income tax rates than the Middle Class or the less extraordinary Upper Class. People at the very top whose average income was about $441,000 EACH DAY paid almost two percent less tax than people who earned $250,000 during the entire year in 2012.[28]

For decades, Republicans have argued that disparity in income and wealth is the price we pay for upward mobility. They claim this inequality is worthwhile because we have greater opportunities in the United States to change our station in life. The chance to work hard, start a business, and get rich is unmatched by any other country in history, or so the story goes. Historians point to Benjamin Franklin and Henry Ford as examples of men who each started with little and became wealthy because of the opportunities available in the United States. While such economic mobility accurately describes our past,

Americans now enjoy less mobility than their peers in Canada, Britain and all of Scandinavia. Countries with robust social safety nets, strong union protection, and truly equal public education have far greater economic mobility than the United States. And contrary to popular belief here in the United States, people in those countries enjoy similar living standards.[29]

Blue Collar Workers, if you want to enjoy living standards equal to the average Western European, reconsider giving your support to some guy who promises everything will be terrific, "believe me, believe me," but refuses to give you any details about how he expects to accomplish his goals. If you want a better country for yourselves and for the average White Collar Worker, stop hating Democrats for giving you those policy details. Stop despising Democrats for being proud of their college degrees. Stop punishing them for using their knowledge of complex issues to explain the reasons for their positions. Stop turning your back on them for using their education to help people.

Do you really want a better country, one that gives you an honest opportunity in life? Good governance takes cooperation, not obstruction, so start voting for Democrats for Congress, not just for president. New laws are initiated in Congress and approved by our president. If you really want to improve the nation, show up for midterm elections in 2018 and help put brakes on the Republican agenda to further enrich the top one percent at your expense. In 2020, vote for the Democratic nominee for president, but expect no progress unless you give that president a Democratic Congress too.

☙❧

7

Conversation with Republicans Regarding Whistles

The 45th president was right about Republican Senator John McCain of Arizona. He is no hero. Wait, that's wrong. Of course the senator was a Vietnam War hero, and that would ring true if all he had done is serve during the war. But he also deserves great respect for the resiliency he demonstrated by enduring captivity and torture, then embarking on a distinguished public career in which he has served his country as few have done in our nation's history. Now, however, he has allowed himself to be captured again, but this time in his own country, by racists who have seized control of the Republican Party.

Racism is nothing new for either major political party in the United States. The Grand Old Party has been blowing a dog whistle to racists for the past 50 years. Richard Nixon's campaign may have started it in 1968 with the "Southern strategy," taking advantage of Southern backlash against Democrats for passing the Civil Rights Act of 1964 and the Voting Rights Act of 1965. Ronald Reagan blew his dog whistle during the 1976 and 1980 presidential campaigns when he repeatedly referred to "strapping young bucks buying T-bone steaks with food stamps" and "Cadillac-driving welfare queens."[1] The phrase *dog whistle politics* is an analogy. Only dogs can hear a real dog whistle because the sound is too high-pitched for human ears. Supposedly, only racists could hear Reagan criticize welfare queens and strapping young bucks on food stamps and understand he really was talking about African Americans. Personally, I question the validity of that analogy. I'm neither dog nor racist nor a member of an obvious minority demographic, but even at the tender age of seventeen, it seemed to me that Candidate Reagan was appealing to white bigots when he criticized "bucks" for using food stamps.

Race baiting continued in 1988. Supporters of George H.W. Bush ran commercials blaming his opponent, Michael Dukakis, for crimes committed by convicted murderer Willie Horton. While on furlough from a Massachusetts prison, Horton raped a white woman and stabbed her fiancée. As governor, Dukakis had vetoed a measure that would have made murderers like Horton ineligible for furlough. The add never mentioned that Horton was African American, but did prominently display his picture.[2] That whistle blasted loud and clear enough for me to hear.

Politicians also are blowing dog whistles when they clamor for tax cuts and states' rights. Medicaid expansion, as encouraged under the Affordable Care Act, illustrates this racial nature of states' rights. Eleven of thirteen Southern states chose not to extend Medicaid to the poor, even though those states would have paid nothing for three years and only 10% of the cost going forward from 2017. When the federal government entrusts safety net programs to states, those with an ugly racial history use them to set a floor that ensures "poor minorities aren't helped, even if that means the poor in general aren't helped," according to Ian Haney Lopez, author of Dog Whistle Politics. Lopez argues that Republican politicians covertly appeal to racism to gain support for laws that enhance corporate profit and increase wealth for the top one percent. The other 99 percent pick up the tab. The result is a rapidly widening wealth gap, continued devastation of the environment, and refusal to address climate change.[3]

During the 2016 presidential campaign, Senator Marco Rubio (R-FL) continued the tradition of blowing on that dog whistle. He attempted to win over racist supporters without offending those of us who try so hard not to be bigots. Marking the 50th anniversary of Lyndon Johnson's anti-poverty speech, he offered this: "I am proposing that we turn over Washington's anti-poverty programs ... to the states."[4] Rubio failed to win over enough voters, probably because he was blowing a dog whistle while another candidate was leaning hard on a train whistle.

Anybody who tries not to be a bigot could hear that whistle blow, but we covered our ears and voted for other candidates. This presidential bid marked the first time a politician had used a racist whistle that should have been audible to everyone, regardless of party, and successfully used it to seize the GOP presidential nomination. There is no need to lay out the case proving that many of his overtures were appeals to racism. Anyone who claims not to see and hear the bigotry is too biased against their opposition to see it, or is just plain lying. This conversation is directed toward the rest — the honest people who did recognize the racist appeals, did not like it, but held their noses and voted for the Republican nominee anyway.

Of course, the racists are not confined to the GOP. Many bigots support Democrats. But as a group, the bigots are singularly responsible for the Republican nominee for president. Decent Republicans, please pay attention.

The Republican nominee won the presidency only with your support. Since you gave him your vote, you made the same mistake many Germans made in 1932 and most Germans continued to make for the ensuing twelve years. Perhaps ours is a bigger error. We have the advantage of hindsight. We know, or should know, how Adolf Hitler exploited the complacency of Germany's decent people to rise to power and murder at least 11 million innocent civilians. We know, or we

119

should recognize, how terrifyingly similar Hitler's scapegoating of Jews and the media was to the 45th president's scapegoating of Mexicans, Muslims and the media — the same media that lavished him with $2 billion of free publicity. Most of us realize by now that neither the Nazi Party nor the Republican Party acted alone. Hitler had Joseph Goebbels to broadcast his racist screed. The 45th president of the United States spread much of his hatred through Twitter, but he had an enormous amount of help from Jeff Sessions, Steve Bannon, and General Michael Flynn. He also had help from Russian cyber warriors who used software bots to weaponize fake news about Hillary Clinton.

We should be taking the proliferation of fake news far more seriously than we seem to be. Fake news kills. Bogus news stories led to the U.S. Civil War and the slaughter of more than 600,000 soldiers, more American deaths than resulted from World Wars I and II combined. Let me elaborate. In debate after debate, candidate Abraham Lincoln stated repeatedly that although he despised the practice of slavery, he did not believe Congress or the President had the Constitutional authority to legislate an end to it. He believed it would die of its own accord as the economy of the South continued to lag the economies of Northern states. Nearly every newspaper throughout the South, however, never reported Lincoln's beliefs or statements that way. They consistently and repeatedly reported that Lincoln proposed to end slavery.

Consequently, South Carolina seceded from the Union only 44 days after the election, which was 74 days before Lincoln's inauguration. Six more southern states — Alabama, Florida, Georgia, Louisiana, Mississippi, and Texas — seceded and formed the Confederate States of America before Lincoln became president. Another four states — Arkansas, North Carolina, Tennessee, and Virginia — joined the Confederacy soon after April 12, 1861, when Confederate troops attacked the Union at Fort Sumter in the harbor of

Charleston, South Carolina. That attack marked the beginning of the Civil War, a war predicated on the lie that Lincoln intended to end slavery, a lie spread by Southern newspapers.

Journalism based on lies, fiction and propaganda is neither new nor unusual anywhere in the world, and certainly not new in the United States. Generally speaking, people have been acting on misrepresentations of facts, misunderstanding of reality, or misreading of political motives for almost the entirety of the United State's existence.

❧

For most of the first nine decades of the Twentieth Century, however, U.S. citizens became better equipped to discern reality from fiction than at any other time in the country's history. Perhaps for the first time ever, they had the opportunity to read reliable facts in a newspaper, hear actual facts on radio, and eventually see real facts on television news programs.

Few people in the United States still dispute that Russia influenced the 2016 presidential election campaign and outcome. Russia paid for the creation and tweeting of fake news. Even former National Security Advisor, Michael Flynn, retweeted some of the nonsense. Russia also hacked emails from the DNC and Hillary Clinton's campaign manager John Podesta, gave the emails to WikiLeaks, which then made them public. Did any of that matter?

Of course it did. Here's proof. This country's public and private institutions overwhelmingly opposed the Republican nominee. He received exactly one endorsement from a major newspaper — the one owned by billionaire casino owner and Republican supporter Sheldon Adelson. Meanwhile hundreds of other major newspapers endorsed Hillary Clinton. Many of those were newspapers that had only endorsed Republicans in the past. USA Today had never endorsed any presidential candidate, but issued an endorsement officially opposing the Republican nominee. The main difference between those media professionals and the average American citizen is that professionals were reading authentic news. Was that a media conspiracy? Russia would like you to believe so. Russian cyber warriors have been hard at work directing our attention to the conspiracy theories so many of us seem to love embracing. President Vladimir Putin's goals are served when citizens of the United States distrust media.

But the media's overwhelming opposition to voting for the Republican nominee was recognition that he was the wrong person for the job. They surmised that he is either wacko, compromised, not knowledgeable enough to even understand the major issues facing our nation, or some scary combination of those shortcomings. Unfortunately, even though nearly 65 million voters got their news from mainstream media that report facts, another 62 million got their fake news from Russia. So, regardless of where Putin was aiming, it's obvious what he killed: American Democracy.

❧ ⚬ ❧

L ike many Americans, I try not to be racist. Nevertheless, we all have, myself included, some implicit bias. I have spent my entire adult life trying to limit my irrational responses, attempting to imagine myself in another person's skin in order to try to empathize with someone coming to entirely different conclusions about life, politics, religion and so on. Whenever I have witnessed politicians using a dog whistle, I reserved my anger for the overt racists and the politicians who covertly appealed to them. I have never been angry at Republican voters who failed to hear the racist whistles blowing. But when the star of the Apprentice became the Republican frontrunner for president, I decided to do something.

I had never volunteered to help a political campaign, never been more involved than simply being a voter. Besides voting, I had not helped Barack Obama or Hillary Clinton in 2008 even though I have always embraced policies that most people call liberal. From my point of view, by the way, *conservative* would be a more accurate label. Having grown up in the 1960's and 70's, I believe integrated schools and equal treatment under the law should be conserved. Portraying diverse characters in entertainment should be conserved, not liberally cast aside. Although preserving these institutions and protections seems natural to me, the 2016 presidential campaign was the first time I felt compelled to offer more than my vote to try to reverse three decades of eroding progressive principles.

In 2000, I voted for Al Gore. I grieved on December 13, 2000, when he finally conceded to George W. Bush. I feared President Bush would appoint Supreme Court justices that would overturn *Roe v. Wade*, walking back decades of women's rights to privacy and to determine the fate of their own bodies. I also feared president Bush's judicial appointees would set back civil rights a few score of years. But I never feared the Bush presidency was an existential threat to humanity. During the 2016 presidential campaign, for the first time in my life, I believed humanity faced such an existential threat from the ambitions of the man who had become the Republican nominee. For the first time in years and years, I sincerely believed everyone who was not a white Christian man born in the United States of America could face violence, imprisonment, government invasion of privacy, illegal search and seizure, even death, if the Republican nominee became president. So I volunteered to help Hillary Clinton's campaign in Colorado.

The campaign season compelled me to cry twice: first, three weeks before the election, then again one week later, ironically, when the polls indicated Hillary Clinton had a 90% chance of winning if the election were held right then. I was crying uncontrollably while canvassing for the Clinton campaign. Was it happiness? After all, the polls showed she was almost certain to win. No, not happiness. Was it relief, the release of anxiety for the passing of an existential threat to humanity? No, not relief. I cried for the passing of America. I cried for the unshakable feeling that everything great about America had died. Not the greatness the Republican nominee spoke of. Not the greatness he believes we lost. But the greatness I believe in.

$$\sim\!\!\infty\!\!\sim$$

The United States of America was a great idea, but did not start out as a great country. The ideals envisioned by the Founders of the country failed to be embodied into the Constitution by its Framers. When those of us born in the 20th and 21st Centuries learn our nation's history, we should never let ourselves be hoodwinked into believing the Framers had created a body of laws that would necessarily lead to a great nation. They had not. Instead, they created a constitution that enshrined the worst aspect of our country: slavery.

They also designed an electoral system that made it improbable the country would ever completely rid itself of slavery's byproduct: racism. Furthermore, they edified slavery in the most cowardly of all possible fashions — without ever mentioning the word. The semantic gymnastics the Framers employed were truly remarkable:

"Representatives and direct Taxes shall be apportioned among the several States which may be included within this Union, according to their respective Numbers, which shall be determined by adding to the whole Number of free Persons, including those bound to Service for a Term of Years, and excluding Indians not taxed, three fifths of all other Persons."

The Framers crafted this clause, part of the third paragraph of Article I, Section 2, to give greater membership in the House of Representatives to states where slaveholding was legal. The Framers also created the Electoral College to give those same slaveholding states greater representation in presidential elections than was reflected by the population of their citizens. This was accomplished by allowing

African Americans to be owned as slaves while withholding citizenship from them, but counting each as three-fifths of a human — all achieved without ever using the word *slave*.

With the ratification of the U.S. Constitution among the several states, the Framers had entirely abandoned the noblest and most often cited clause in the Declaration of Independence:

"... all Men are created equal ..."

During those early days of the United States, voters had to be white men who owned land. Women had no voting rights. Neither did African-American slaves, Native Americans, or anyone under age twenty-one. In other words, a person had to be relatively rich, white, male, and over 21 years old to vote. Great is not a word to accurately describe that set of conditions.

Meanwhile, the First Amendment to the Constitution guaranteed the right of the same rich, white, males to spread unlimited propaganda throughout the land. "Congress shall make no law ... abridging the freedom ... of press ..."[1] The Amendment does not prevent poor or middle-income people from freely using the press. Being less than rich accomplished that, and still maintains that restriction, even in the age of the Internet and social media such as Facebook, Twitter, Snapchat, and YouTube — especially in the age of social media.

But throughout two centuries since the Constitution was ratified, one group after another has gained access to due process and equal protection of the laws. First, non-property owners gained the right to vote. Then African Americans, Native Americans, women, Asian Americans, and 18-year olds each in their turn received the right to vote. African-American and Latino-American children received the right to an equal public education. Women gained full rights to make their own reproductive choices. People with disabilities gained access

---

[1] United States Constitution. "Congress shall make no law respecting an establishment of religion, or prohibiting the free exercise thereof; or abridging the freedom of speech, or of the press, or the right of the people peaceably to assemble, and to petition the Government for a redress of grievances."

to everything, even buildings. Finally, people who are lesbian, gay, bisexual, transgender or queer acquired the right to marry. We often view these rights as having been given to these various groups of people by Congress, presidents, or the Supreme Court.

In truth, due process and equal protection of the laws are rights that were taken, not given. Minorities and women tenaciously fought for and demanded their rights. They were gained through protests, petitions, assembly, speech, plans made in churches, and through access to the press and other news media. Though the Constitution did not guarantee citizenship, due process, or equal protection to everyone, the First Amendment did contain just enough protection to give every minority a sliver of hope. Those hopes have become reality for virtually every diverse group of people in our country.

That is the greatness I believe in.

$$\infty \, \infty$$

I am so much less bothered by the 45th president than I am by the 62 million Americans who voted for him. The GOP has, in my humble opinion, relinquished any right it ever had to expect to be treated with dignity. If you voted for the 45th president, you may have been hoodwinked by fake news, you may have been obsessed with Hillary Clinton's emails that contained zero classified documents, you may believe global climate change is a Chinese hoax or that evolution is not a scientific fact. But surely you realize it's not okay to trash African Americans, Latinos, women, and handicapped people. You could not believe those attitudes are acceptable unless... Well, we simply should not believe those attitudes are acceptable.

Surely you cannot believe it was okay for the Republican nominee to lie about how the economy works, the effects of trade policies, his tax returns, his treasonous investment in Cuba, and his investments within America's rival nations. If you've read this far, I'll assume you're not an overt bigot. The only possible justification left for electing this president would be that your vote represents your stance on only one issue: taking away a woman's right to choose to have an abortion. Regardless of the reasons for your vote, you surely know by now: All the bad news about Hillary Clinton was fake; all the disgusting facts about the Republican nominee came right out of his mouth. How could people vote for him without feeling ashamed?

‹๑๑๑๑›

December 2, 2016, the president elect took a phone call from the president of Taiwan and the uproar throughout the country lasted two days. Some background might be helpful here. China, officially called The People's Republic of China, does not recognize Taiwan's sovereignty. China insists the island nation is a wayward province belonging to the PRC. Ever since Richard Nixon became the first U.S. president to visit China, our policy had been that we do recognize Taiwan's sovereignty, we maintain diplomatic ties, and to this day, we continue our two-way trade relationship. But to enable China to save face, our presidents do not negotiate or even talk directly to Taiwan's presidents. When the U.S. president elect accepted the phone call in late 2016, political pundits said he was a buffoon. But he and his posse defended the contact as nothing more than a harmless courtesy call. Two days later, though, his posse had a new story to tell. The Washington Post reported:

"This historic communication ... was the product of months of quiet preparations and deliberations among [the president elect's] advisers about a new strategy for engagement with Taiwan that began even before he became the Republican presidential nominee... The call also reflects the views of hard-line advisers urging [the president elect] to take a tough opening line with China."5 That was interesting spin, but no one ever explained why the president elect had told a very different story two days earlier.

Meanwhile, whatever the excuse for this apparent gaff, he continues to avoid seeking advice from U.S. State Department personnel. These are people who could have warned him of the four-decade-old policy of U.S. presidents refraining from direct communications with any president of Taiwan. That long-entrenched policy was an attempt to woo the People's Republic of China to do business with the United States and to encourage the development of a free-market economy within China even while the Communist Party maintains absolute control over government. The policy worked.

Apparently, it worked too well, because during his campaign for president, the Republican nominee repeatedly bemoaned, "China is killing us!" He was talking about China's trade surplus as compared to the U.S. trade deficit. It was hard to take him seriously, though. After all, a trade surplus or deficit has no direct relationship with the well-being of a country's economy. Besides, the candidate also said, "Mexico is killing us!" and "Japan is killing us!" Anybody who pays attention to world affairs knows Mexico is nearly a failed state, with drug cartels that murder police officers, judges, and anyone else who interferes with their illicit businesses. And Japan has been in or near economic recession for eighteen years.

But it was especially hard to take the Republican nominee seriously about China. This is a country that has implemented reforms almost exactly as our country would have hoped. Without revolution, the government chose to abandon communist policies and embrace a free-market economy. According to The World Bank in September, 2016, "Since initiating market reforms in 1978, China ... has experienced rapid economic and social development. [Gross Domestic Product] growth has averaged nearly 10 percent a year — the fastest sustained expansion by a major economy in history — and has lifted more than 800 million people out of poverty."[6]

What more could the United States ask for?

Well, for one, freedom-loving people could wish China were not building artificial islands in international waters off the coasts of Vietnam, Malaysia and the Philippines and claiming them as new territory.[7] A person with a really good brain, like the 45th president claims to have, would devise a shrewd plan to give the United States a nonconfrontational excuse to order Navy vessels to routinely navigate those waters. A president who was forward looking, cautious, and able to anticipate every move a rival might make, that president would invite all the smaller nations surrounding those disputed waters to enter into a trade agreement favorable to all parties, but which diminishes the power and influence of China. In short, a president such as Barack Obama would have his secretaries of the State Department, first Hillary Clinton then John Kerry, lay the groundwork and negotiate the Trans-Pacific Partnership.

Unfortunately, neither the 45th president nor Bernie Sanders are shrewd. So, with their one-two punches, they sold the American public on the notion that the proliferation of international trade agreements was the major reason for the loss of high-paying manufacturing jobs. The truth? Since 1990, most of the manufacturing jobs disappearing around the world, not just in the United States, were lost to automation or other technological improvements. Machines are doing the work humans used to perform on assembly lines and grocery lines. By the time Bernie Sanders was through with his campaign, not only had he convinced Democratic voters the TPP was evil, he had convinced Hillary Clinton she had to drop support for the agreement in order to win the Oval Office. She withdrew her support. But she will not be moving back into the White House any time soon.

And the 45th president? Apparently too arrogant to admit a mistake, he pretends he took the call from President Tsai Ing-wen after deliberate calculation. He and his posse and the unwitting media are too busy cleaning up his mess, making that phone call look like a good idea, to see or understand the elegance of the TPP. He is blind to its ability to allow the United States to insert itself into a part of the world where it enjoys little influence. He does not understand how the agreement enables his country to credibly claim its only interest in patrolling the area is to ensure the continuation of free commerce.

No. This is way too subtle for the man with the great brain. His methods — mistakenly taking the wrong call, lying about the reasons for two days, then concocting a story about how he was the genius behind the manipulation — are the methods we powerless citizens will have to get used to for the next four years. Even worse, his posse now tells the lies for him, normalizing his behavior.

ॐ

Extremism has also been normalized in the Republican Party. For example, although Republicans are partially correct about problems caused by immigration, party leadership suggests inhumane solutions that are completely unnecessary. Immigration is dampening the ability of our workers to earn a decent wage. Better solutions are available, however, than blaming undocumented workers and deporting people who have never known life in another country.

Undocumented Mexican immigration, which declined during President Obama's tenure, is a drag on U.S. workers only when employers exploit the immigrants' fear of deportation to illegally pay below-minimum wages. This has the same effect on our economy as slavery did in Southern states before the Civil War. Poor white laborers were competing against unpaid slaves, which put tremendous downward pressure on a free person's wages. To eliminate similar drag on wages for today's U.S. workers, the undocumented must obtain documents. The solution is actually that simple.

Giving them citizenship is not necessary and not even a good idea. Conferring citizenship would encourage future waves of illegal immigration. To wit: Ronald Reagan's amnesty program led to the current problem. I do believe we should offer citizenship to any legal residents who serve in the military, just as we did in 1919 to Native Americans who had served during World War I.

Nevertheless, many of these undocumented Mexican citizens were infants when their parents brought them to the United States. They did not make this choice for themselves, and they have never known another country. We should give them residency and work status so their presence among the workforce stops putting downward pressure on everyone's wages. That also would allow them to proceed with their lives without fear of deportation. Furthermore, although they would never enjoy the rights and benefits of citizenship, their children born in the United States automatically would.[8]

A bit more about the economic impact of undocumented workers: Many people get upset because undocumented laborers pay no taxes. But they do. Obviously, they pay sales taxes, and directly or indirectly, they pay property taxes. Most even pay social security tax and income tax, and ironically, never file returns to receive any of the refunds they are entitled to. In fact, undocumented workers contribute as much or more to the economy than many citizens. They are consumers who buy food, medicine, clothing, shelter, and smartphones. Every time they make a purchase, they help employ a citizen.

People typically misunderstand this about economics; they believe there are a fixed number of jobs. Actually, the number of jobs generally expands to accommodate the number of people. Simply put, anybody who consumes is a job creator. Your consumption of education pays my salary; my consumption of lamb chops pays the meat cutter's salary, and so on. But we all do better when the people making the least amount of money get a raise. When they make more, they spend more, which helps employ somebody new.

We should welcome any measure that raises minimum wage, or at least stops downward pressure on wages. One step we could take would be to eliminate the H-1B visa program, which is little more than welfare for corporations. In theory, the program allows employers to import laborers who fill jobs for which there are no qualified citizens to hire. In practice, H-1B displaces American workers and forces some to accept lower wages than the market would otherwise pay for their skills.[9] We are helping corporations import cheap foreign labor to supplant American workers. The primary benefit is that corporations reap greater profit. That profit becomes money that rarely leaves the accounts of the already wealthy, almost never circulates through the economy, and completely fails to create new jobs.

❦

One area of our economy that would benefit from downward wage pressure, though, would be health care. A measure we could take to improve life in the United States would be to allow increased immigration by doctors, cutting the cost of medical practitioners. This is basic supply and demand. An insufficient supply of doctors for the past forty years has yielded higher salaries. U.S. medical doctors earn double the average income of comparable doctors worldwide, with general practitioners earning 36% more than GP's in the second-ranked country, the United Kingdom.[10] Those higher salaries result in greater healthcare costs for consumers. If we allowed more foreign doctors to immigrate to the United States, residents would get truly affordable healthcare.

❦

Immigration reform can never solve the country's biggest problem: racial distrust, even hatred. This exists on such a grand scale that it literally kills us. As noted in Chapter 4: *Conversation with Americans Regarding Terrorism*, an African-American man gunned down five innocent police officers in Dallas, Texas on July 7, 2016. This was revenge, Micah Xavier Johnson said, for innocent black lives snuffed out by police and vigilantes in recent years. A year earlier, Dylann Roof murdered nine innocent African-American church goers.

We could continue looking for ways to retaliate, place blame, and punish, or we could look for solutions.

For instance, we could, as Martin Luther King, Jr. implored, continue striving to build a nation where our children "...will not be judged by the color of their skin but by the content of their character." Every person in the United States wishing for racial harmony, peace, justice, and a more prosperous society should be wondering why segregation persists in public schools. In an atmosphere teeming with pundits and politicians screaming at each other, integrating schools might seem trivial or puny. Experts thunder about moral questions such as whether Black Lives Matter or Blue Lives Matter. Community leaders debate gun laws. They propose improved training for police officers. Some suggest longer prison sentences; others want shorter prison sentences. We question whether any new action will ever solve the problems generated by racism in our country.

Nevertheless, a solution has existed since 1954. In *Brown v. Board of Education of Topeka* [Kansas], the Supreme Court unanimously decided school segregation was responsible for perpetuating racial inequality in our country. Of greater legal significance, it violated the 14th Amendment to the Constitution. In addition to granting citizenship to former slaves born on U.S. soil, that post Civil War amendment prohibits any state from denying "to any person within its jurisdiction the equal protection of the laws." On behalf of the court's unanimous decision, Chief Justice Earl Warren wrote that African-American children attending segregated public schools were not receiving an equal education even if the resources available were identical to those in whites-only schools. "To separate them (African Americans) from others of similar age and qualifications solely because of their race generates a feeling of inferiority as to their status in the community that may affect their hearts and minds in a way unlikely ever to be undone."[11]

This legal conclusion was based on scientific findings entered into evidence in *Briggs v. Elliott* (South Carolina), one of five cases that

133

had been combined for consideration under *Brown*. In the "Doll Test" study, Psychologists Kenneth and Mamie Clark used four dolls, identical except for color. They showed them to black children between age three and seven and asked questions to determine preference. The majority selected the white doll and attributed positive characteristics to it. The Clarks also gave the children outline drawings of a boy and girl and asked them to color the figures the same color as themselves. Many of the children with dark complexions colored the figures with a white or yellow crayon. The Clarks concluded that "prejudice, discrimination, and segregation" caused black children to develop a sense of inferiority and self-hatred.[12]

During the 20 years following *Brown*, federal courts ordered cities and states to integrate schools. Unfortunately, the new dynamic lasted only fifteen to twenty years, depending upon location. Just one generation grew up going to school with people of different color. Beginning in the early 1990's, communities all over the country invented a multitude of methods for circumventing the legal requirement to integrate public schools. Now we have two newer generations who have grown up nearly as segregated as were my parents and every generation of Americans preceding them.

The preferred method for enabling continued segregation is called school choice — another dog whistle. If your ears are not attenuated to high-pitched racial overtones, school choice simply enables you to enroll your children in the best public school to which you are willing to drive them. This is open to everyone, regardless of race, religion, color or ethnicity. If you're poverty stricken, however, this choice is an illusion. You might not own a car. You might be a single working parent. You might be disabled, but whatever the reason, you are unable to drive your children across town to a different school. If you are African American or Latino, you are at least twice as likely to fall below the official poverty line, twice as likely to have no school choices, despite any illusion to the contrary. That is how school choice negatively impacts minorities more than the white majority in the United States.

The practical effect of school choice is that people a little higher up the socioeconomic ladder take their children to better schools with more experienced, higher paid teachers. The neighborhood schools they flee are left with the poorest students from the most disadvantaged homes. Most teachers would rather work at schools whose students do not come bundled together with a host of issues that frequently accompany poverty. When they accumulate enough experience to achieve seniority, they transfer to schools with a richer population. Inevitably, the schools they abandon replace them with teachers who have less experience or no experience at all, perpetuating the schools' inferiority. So goes the evil cycle of school choice.

Schools in poverty-stricken neighborhoods, despite a host of funding schemes, federal grants, and laws designed to overcome deficient resources, almost always operate with less money than schools elsewhere. Furthermore, that physical, palpable inequality pales in comparison to the psychological damage revealed by the doll test. The solution, of course, is to integrate public schools again.

∞

I have a scheme to engineer integration in a way that would still allow parents to choose the schools their children attend. To my dismay, the public charter school where I have taught for the past fourteen years has few minority students, so I have thought much about how to achieve a mix of students that reflects the diversity of our nation's population, preserves school choice, even extends choices to the poorest people in our communities.

In most districts, students are worth a fixed amount of money to the schools they attend. In other words, the school a child attends receives a fixed sum of money from the district to pay for that child's enrollment in the school. Put even more simply, the school's budget is dependent upon the number of students enrolled. In the district where I teach, our schools receive about $7,000 per student each year.

Our elementary school has close to 500 students, so we get about $3.5 million per year for our operating budget. If our enrollment decreased by forty students one year, a bit over two students per classroom, we would lose about $280,000 that year. That gives us great incentive to try to keep our students and their parents happy.

For most families, this system works fairly well. For some, it's a little inconvenient. People who live too far away to have their children walk, must drive them to school instead. But most poor people who live outside walking distance simply cannot get their children to our school. I used to teach at a Denver (Colorado) Public School that achieved integration by busing in children from all over the city. Every morning, more than thirty busses delivered most of the student body to our doors, and every afternoon, they took the children back to their neighborhoods. The story of how funds are provided for that extraordinary amount of transportation is a long one, complex, and does not merit a full explanation here. The Denver Public School district provides that money for only the one elementary school, so obviously, this example could not solve the nation's wider problem. The point, however, is that integrating the school is possible when there is enough money.

Fortunately, enough money exists. The school districts already have it available, but to make my scheme work, they must reallocate funds a bit. They would have to increase the amount of money schools receive for students living in poverty. Nationwide, that is a little fewer than 20 percent of children.[13] Those students would carry with them, so to speak, ten percent more money. The money would go to their school, of course.

To pay for that increase, schools would have to receive about 2.5 percent less funding for each student not living in poverty. Please note, this is a color-blind policy. The financial adjustment is associated with poverty, not race, religion, or color. Students above the poverty line in my district would confer to their schools $175 less per year than they do now. Students below the poverty line would confer $700 extra, which could easily pay for transporting them to schools outside their neighborhoods if their families made that choice. The national average of such transportation was $452 per student in 2013.[14] The extra money also would cover additional fees most schools charge, but which they rarely collect from poverty-stricken students.

Under that scheme, a district expends the same total amount of money. Some schools would receive less funding — schools that have few or no students who live in poverty. Other schools would receive more — those with a high proportion of children living in poverty. Those schools may have to provide transportation for a few new students, but they will have more than enough money to do so. Many people living in poverty likely would choose to have their children remain in their neighborhood schools. Those schools, after all, would receive a sudden windfall of extra money to be invested in better educational resources. That could mean new books, technology, smaller classes — whatever their administrators decide are priorities. Regardless of their choices, schools would have to create successful environments for their students. Otherwise, students leave and the funds would dwindle.

Some school administrators would implement strategies to deliberately appeal to poor students because, in this alternate world, poor students bring more money to the school. People all over the country probably would be more inclined to approve tax increases for school funding. Currently, most parents have little incentive to seek more money for public school funding. In the opinions of most parents, the education their children receive is just fine.[15] But if their neighborhood school suddenly lost nearly ten percent of its funding, they would see the picture differently.

The benefits would accrue to all of society. We would begin to acquire the salve we need to heal wounds that have festered for three centuries. Our children should grow up living and going to school among fellow humans who might believe in a different religion or who happen to have different skin color. We should live among people with different definitions for a bad hair day, expose ourselves to people who express themselves with their own style of clothes, or listen to different music. After a single generation, we would receive the benefit of acquiring knowledge and culture from many groups of people. Better yet, we would also learn how much we have in common with each other. In short, we would be greater than we are now, greater than we have ever been, by living the ideals set forth in the Declaration of Independence and dreamed of by Martin Luther King, Jr.

8

Conversation with Southerners

Imagine no Israel. Pretend Jews never declared the existence of the country in 1948 because they returned to Germany after the end of World War II. The few who survived German concentration camps and death camps stayed in the country. Those who survived Nazi camps in Poland, Austria, France, and the Netherlands moved to Germany too. Pretend the 300,000 survivors from those camps and others never moved to Palestine during and shortly after the war. Instead, one way or another, all ended up in Germany. By the mid 1960's, the Jewish population would have been about 2.6 million in Germany instead of a mere 200,000.

❦

Now imagine Gregor, age ten, a blonde, blue-eyed German boy. One day his father begins telling him about his grandfather's service during the war. His grandpa, his opa, was a bomber pilot, assigned to Eagle Squadron in command of aircraft

Ju88 U4+TK.* Gregor's opa starting flying missions in January of 1940 when Gregor's father was only seven years old. On April 9, Opa and the flight crews of the other 46 planes comprising Eagle Squadron were ordered to leave their base on the northwest German island of Sylt and fly north toward Norway. They were accompanied by 41 more bombers. Their mission was to engage a large British Royal Navy fleet that German scouts had sighted southwest of Bergen. So began the Nazi invasion of Norway.

As Opa flew his Ju88 into battle, his navigator pointed and tried to out-shout the roaring engines, "Look over there! Ten o'clock low!" Opa looked out the portside window and saw where his navigator was pointing. Sailing by itself, removed from the protection of the rest of the fleet, was His Majesty's Ship Gurkha, a Tribal-class British destroyer designed for speed and power. The ship had maneuvered away from the fleet to find a better position for firing against the Luftwaffe's onslaught. This left the Gurkha vulnerable.

Opa turned his craft toward the destroyer and instantly learned why the Gurkha's commander had the confidence to leave the fleet. The Destroyer was outfitted with a heavy contingent of guns designed specifically for battle against aircraft.

As the bomber bore down on HMS Gurkha, Opa heard a sound like a freight train roaring past his left ear. That was anti-aircraft fire almost 5-inches thick. A near miss, and seconds later another near miss, this time on the starboard side. The Gurkha's gunners were firing machine gun rounds at the aircraft too. Opa's bombardier fired back at the destroyer with his mounted gun, but Opa pulled back on

---

* This plane lasted only 140 days beginning January 2, 1940. In late March, the plane was part of a squadron using the frozen Lake Jonsvatnet in Norway as an airfield. On April 21, 1940, the plane slipped beneath the surface of the melting lake. The German Luftwaffe abandoned the plane, and soon, the lake had swallowed it whole. The Ju88 U4+TK was recovered from Lake Jonsvatnet in Norway and restored from 2005 through 2013. The recovery team discovered two bullet holes in the navigator's seat. http://www.ju88.net/

the control wheel, trying to climb out of harm's way. A third round passed so close to the fuselage it shook the craft.

Soon, three other Ju88's joined Opa, all firing guns at the British ship. The ship fired back. Another round thundered past, then exploded into the plane flying near their starboard side. That was the first loss from their squadron.

But Opa kept climbing and within seconds, the big guns couldn't climb with him. The anti-aircraft guns couldn't be raised past 40 degrees. Machine gun fire could reach them, but it would take a lot of rounds or very lucky placement to bring down Opa's plane with bullets from a machine gun. Soon the plane would be passing over the British ship. The bombardier waited until they were right above the destroyer. Then he let go, just as bullets pierced the plane. The half-ton bomb fell away beneath them.

One bomb was all it took.

The Gurkha took a direct hit to the engine room. Soon, the ship was aflame and immobile. Most of its crew members were rescued by a British cruiser, but sixteen British sailors, trapped behind the fire, burned alive. Fire eventually engulfed the destroyer, and it sank off the coast of Bergen.[1]

Opa's plane survived the day, but two of the Gurkha's last machine gun rounds hit the navigator. One pierced his hip, the other ripped through his rib cage, his heart, and scapula, and lodged into the seat behind him. He died in seconds. All together, the Luftwaffe lost 17 airmen that day. The Fatherland also lost four Ju88's from Eagle squadron. It had been the largest air-sea battle of the war so far.

Opa and his squadron returned to their base on Sylt, but the following day they received orders to relocate their base to Jonsvatnet, a tiny frozen lake near Trondheim, Norway. From there, they staged attacks on Norwegian cities further north. But with advancing warm weather, the lake was thawing. Planes could land only late at night and had to take off early the next morning. When opa and his crew landed the night of April 21st, a wheel broke through the ice. Though the crew was uninjured, the plane could not be salvaged. With the frozen lake melting, just twelve days after arriving at Jonsvatnet they abandoned the base and Opa's Ju88, which eventually broke through the ice completely and sank to the bottom.

Opa and his crew were assigned to a new craft, another Ju88, and they helped their countrymen defeat Norway by June of that same year. They remained in Norway, defending the German position and attacking convoys that were taking supplies from Iceland, North America, and the United Kingdom through the arctic ocean to the Soviet Union. They were stationed far north at the port of Narvik.

On May 25, 1942, Opa and his crew were ordered to fly northwest and intercept one of these Arctic Convoys. They soon sighted the flotilla, 35 merchant ships carrying supplies to their enemies, escorted by five destroyers and ten other ships of war. Opa fixed his sights on HMS Ashanti. This was another Tribal destroyer, just like the one his crew had sunk two years earlier. He liked the idea of fighting against the same type of craft that had marked his battle baptism.

So he brought up the nose of his Ju88 and started climbing. When he was certain he had surpassed a forty-degree angle from the deck of the Ashanti, he turned toward it, intent on its destruction. Within a half minute, the ship was two miles away and 24,000 feet below.

"We will be in bombing position in twenty-four seconds," the navigator announces.

"What is this?" the bombardier asks while looking through binoculars.

"What?" Opa asks.

The Bombardier hands his binoculars up to Opa. "Look at the guns on the starboard side."

Opa puts the glasses to his eyes. On the starboard side is a pair of anti-aircraft guns rotating to face his armada of planes. Three other pairs of guns also are spinning to face his fleet. After his crew sank the Gurkha, Britain refitted all their remaining Tribals with twin anti-aircraft guns able to fire 80 degrees above horizontal. Now, one set of twins is tilting upward until each of the two barrels seem to be pointed right at Opa.

A moment later a puff of smoke blasts from each of the two guns. Opa slams the control wheel forward. Instantly, the plane dives, rapidly picking up speed. On the Ashanti, all six of the other anti-aircraft guns fire. In five seconds, they all blast again. At that same moment, four other destroyers fire their weapons. It will be another few seconds before the first shells arrive, but Opa has no way of knowing exactly where they have been aimed.

He pulls back on the control wheel and levels the plane. Then they're hit.

Gregor cries as his father finishes the story, his pride swelling for Opa, the grandpa who sacrificed his life for the fatherland.

✥

So imagine how Gregor, to honor Opa, finds and buys the perfect shirt. It's bright red with a big circular field of white, and a black swastika in the center of the circle. He wears his new shirt everywhere. Many of his friends wear similar apparel. Some even have swastikas tattooed on their arms. Lots of Germans display Nazi flags outside their houses. They honor their fathers and their grandfathers, brave men who fought in the war.

And imagine Gregor's surprise one Saturday afternoon when he rides his bicycle into a new neighborhood and instantly notices an odd atmosphere, a different feel to the place. None of the houses display flags. Nearly all the men are wearing knitted beanies. The women wear wigs. Everyone he passes on the street, adults and children alike, turn and glare at him. Finally, as he approaches a middle-aged man whose eyes are practically boring into him, Gregor hits his brakes. As he stands on the street, legs straddling the bike, hands leaning on handlebars, he asks, "What is the matter with everyone?"

"What's the matter, you ask?" says the man.

"Yah, why is everyone staring at me?"

"Why are they staring?"

"Would you please stop repeating everything I say?" Gregor says, then he continues, "Why does everyone in this neighborhood keep pointing at me and whispering to each other. Do you have some problem with me?"

"It's your shirt, young man."

Gregor looks down to remind himself what he's wearing. "What's wrong with this shirt?"

"What's wrong! What's wrong? It has a swastika!"

"So? It was our national symbol. I display it to honor my opa who died in the war."

"Yah," the man agrees, "many died in the war. Six million Jews died. Both my opas and omas died, my papa, mama, my sister. None were soldiers, but they all died in the war anyway."

"Oh gosh, I'm sorry," Gregor says.

"My opas and parents starved to death in the camps, but not my sister. Rose had withered to a wisp by the winter of 1944, but she was still alive. Herr Hitler murdered her in the gas chamber."

"But most German soldiers knew nothing of the gas chambers!" Gregor protests.

"Yah, but now they know. To us," he sweeps his hand around to indicate the people of his neighborhood, "the swastika is a symbol of death, extermination, genocide."

"That's not true at all! The swastika is not about gas chambers or death camps. It's a symbol of bravery and sacrifice and honor."

"No, young man. For us, it is a reminder of murder at the hands of our own countrymen."

Imagine 2.6 million Jewish people living in Germany, trying to explain to their fellow countrymen why they are terrified of anyone wearing a swastika. Whenever they leave their neighborhoods to do business with the government, to attend a concert, or see a play, they pass through street after street where houses proudly display flags honoring the people who murdered their families.

You must use your imagination to see that. Nobody could have witnessed it in the real Germany of 1965. Almost no Germans ever displayed swastikas after World War II. They were far too ashamed of their collective actions as a nation. As they learned of the atrocities of the Holocaust, they required their children to learn about them too, in school and in church. They may have been proud of their parents and grandparents who loved their country and fought in the war. Nevertheless, they were far too aware of the guilt they shared for the murder of six million Jews and five million others, all innocent. Eleven million people, all non-combatants, were rounded up, and herded into camps. About half died from the conditions and their treatment in those camps. Most of the rest were marched into chambers and murdered with poison gas.

In the real Germany, you do not see many swastikas.

Imagine being black and living in the Southern United States. If you took the title of this chapter seriously, you might not have to imagine. You might be African American. If not, I am begging you to imagine what it is like for black children in the South to ride their bicycles outside their neighborhoods. Imagine pedaling along streets and seeing cars with license plates flaunting the battle flag that celebrates their ancestors' slavery. Riding downtown, they see that same battle flag waving proudly, defiantly, over their government buildings and in their public parks. Everywhere they go, they see a flag that glorifies the rape, torture and murder of their ancestors.

Most people who display that flag see it as a symbol of their own ancestors' bravery in fighting for the Confederacy, fighting for its cause. But that cause was the most horrific aspect of our nation's history. The rest of us see a whole swath of our country clinging to the worst part of our past and honoring that. We see a battle flag that should have been retired forever in April of 1865. Instead, the White Knights of the Ku Klux Klan have used it to inflict terror for the better part of 150 years. State and municipal governments have used it as a symbol of defiance while continuing to deny basic human rights and citizenship rights to their African-American citizens.

Therein lies the biggest difference between Germany and the United States. Germans are rightly ashamed their country perpetrated the Jewish Holocaust. They are committed to ensuring nothing like it ever happens again. They are sensitive to their nation's victims, to the few who miraculously survived, and to the descendents of their victims.

Many white Southerners apparently feel no shame for the African-American Holocaust. They seem to take no responsibility for ensuring that descendents of their forefathers' victims can proceed with life, liberty and the pursuit of happiness. Why do so many white Southerners continue to flaunt Civil War battle flags, then deny that such a display amounts to terrorism inflicted upon their black neighbors? I do not expect anyone to answer for the sins of their forefathers. What most decent people hope is that white Americans will recognize their own sins and end this 150-year long campaign of terror against fellow citizens.

9

Conversations with Gary Johnson and Bill Weld

ary Johnson: Obviously, you feel underappreciated and under recognized, otherwise, why would you run for President of the United States on the Libertarian ticket, which had no chance of doing anything other than handing the presidency to the Republican? So this is for you, Gary, so you can feel like you have been recognized, and haven't been ignored: Hello, Gary!

◦ ◦ ◦

ill Weld: You didn't do enough, dude. What was that nonsense in the last two weeks before the November 8 election? "If you're voting for one of the two major parties, don't vote for [the Republican nominee]."

If you believed what you were saying, how can you justify the fact that you neglected to say, "Don't vote for Gary and me under any circumstance! You really need to cast off this existential threat to humanity and vote for Hillary Clinton. Supporters, this is no joke. The

Republican nominee says, 'I alone can fix it,' as though he's Jesus, but the real savior this year is Hillary Clinton. You must vote for her. Not the Republican. Not me and Gary. Not anyone else. Every negative you've ever heard or read about Hillary Clinton is a lie, and every outrageous story you've ever heard about this Republican nominee is absolutely true, came out of his own mouth, and should scare the Bejeezus out of you! And you absolutely must get out and vote!"

That's what you should've said, Bill.

10

Conversation with Bernie Bros

D udes, I love Bernie Sanders as much as anyone does, so honestly, I'm mystified. How could so many of you choose to abandon his goals when it came to the general election? Some of you failed to vote. Some voted for Gary Johnson, others for Jill Stein. A few of you even voted for, and helped deliver to the White House, the guy with an inability to find anything wrong with Vladimir Putin. So in pursuit of perfection, you sentenced the United States to decades of Neil Gorsuch serving on the Supreme Court instead of Merrick Garland.

Our entire country must now suffer, perhaps for a generation, perhaps forever, the consequences of the electorate's need for purity. Senator Sanders and Hillary Clinton hold basically the same views on nearly every policy issue. The two of them have almost identical goals for our country. There are differences, but these are less about direction and more a question of degree.

Sure, he wanted to raise the minimum wage to $15 per hour, while she supported an increase to only $12 per hour. Granted, even though that was in line with a bill under consideration in Congress in 2016, her goal was undeniably less ambitious. Also, as a senator, Clinton voted to authorize war against Saddam Hussein in Iraq, a vote she subsequently decided had been a mistake and for which she apologized. This is one of the main reasons I supported Secretary Clinton — her willingness to admit a mistake in the face of evidence. Hell, that is the quality that distinguishes us most from Republicans. Sometimes we are willing to accept evidence even when it refutes our mistaken beliefs.

⚬⚬

Many people look for leaders who are rock solid, embrace the right views, and maintain those views for a lifetime. Senator Sanders appears to be just such a leader. He has been railing against giant corporations and wealth inequality his entire career. Those unyielding views were among the main reasons I originally supported his candidacy. I even told a canvasser I would be voting for him in the Colorado caucus. I meant it too, but as it turned out, I voted for Hillary Clinton in that caucus. Man, was I in the minority there! Bernie won the Colorado caucus in a landslide.

The reason I changed my mind just before that caucus was that Senator Sanders seemed too unyielding, too attached to his beliefs, less interested in facts and evidence. One main problem was his stance on trade agreements, which I addressed in Chapter 6: *Conversation with Blue Collar Workers*. Another big concern for me was his proposal for free college tuition. While I absolutely do believe the government should pay for a qualified student's tuition to college, any discussion of such a proposal is ridiculously premature — not because it is politically untenable, nor because it would require tax increases, though those arguments are true. No, the problem with free college is that it would be unfair to poor people. They would be partly responsible for paying those increased taxes, but unable to fully share in the benefits.

Senator Sanders is correct that many first-world countries manage to pay tuition for their qualified candidates to attend college. In New Zealand, for one example, as long as a student continues to have grades demonstrating an ability to succeed, the government continues to subsidize that student's advancement through college, through graduate programs, even through doctoral programs.

In order to pay for publicly funded college, New Zealand limits scholarships to students who have demonstrated the ability to succeed. The problem with such a limitation in our country would be that a disproportionate number of poor Latino and African-American citizens have been shut out of fair opportunities to receive an excellent education prior to college. Poor white people also have been shut out. They should not have to shoulder any part of the burden of paying college tuition for people who received more than their fair share of educational funding in pre-kindergarten through 12th grade. We must address pre-k through 12th-grade education before we offer free college tuition. This is the only course that would be fair to people who have been disadvantaged by centuries of racism, or by their parents' poverty.

The final problem I had with Senator Sanders was his proposal for healthcare reform. His numbers didn't add up. I admire him for proposing a single-payer health plan even though the political environment seems to make the prospect of passing such legislation improbable. In politics, sometimes we have to aim for what we think is best, hoping to at least end up with policy that is better than what we have now. But according to Nobel Prize winning economist Paul Krugman, the Sanders plan assumes huge cost savings that are unlikely, considering its promises of more coverage than Medicare and greater coverage than single-payer systems in other countries. "This lets Sanders claim he could make it work with much lower taxes on the Middle Class than probably would be needed."[1]

But let's not just blindly trust Paul Krugman. According to the Senator's website, his plan would cost less than $39 per month for a family of four whose income is $50,000. Sign me up! His total plan would raise $1.38 trillion in taxes from businesses and households. Those taxes would be earmarked to pay for all the costs of health care currently paid by private citizens and industry.[2] In 2015, that expense was $1.73 trillion,[3] which would leave $350 billion unfunded. That shortfall, according to Sanders, would no longer be needed because it represents profits earned by private insurance companies that would no longer exist.

My math tells a different story. In 2015, private health insurance companies spent $1.072 trillion in payments for health services.[4] Their profit margin was about 9%,[5] so they earned close to $106 billion, which still leaves a $244 billion shortfall in the senator's plan. That works out to an extra $254 per month for the family of four that Senator Sanders writes about on his website. But that number still underestimates the total cost.

With a single-payer system — let's go with Senator Sanders on this and call it Medicare For All — truly everyone would be covered, which is fantastic. That would put 28.5 million[6] more people on the new insurance plan, probably increasing costs by at least $197 billion. That amounts to about $205 per month for that family of four. Now their expense has increased to $5,868 per year. Add to that amount an unknown cost due to the new plan having zero co-pays and zero deductibles, which would give people incentive to exercise zero restraint when making appointments to visit their doctors. That puts the upward pressure on costs Krugman warned us about.

Even considering the costs Senator Sanders left out, Medicare for All still may be a great idea. I would support it with a few tweaks. For instance, a co-pay for visits to healthcare professionals would help give patients an incentive to remain personally responsible for doing what they can to stay healthy — avoid tobacco, excessive consumption of liquor, bad food, and so on. The amount of co-pay could be means tested: It would depend upon the patient's income and ability to pay.

My point about this proposal, however, is that the Senator promised far, far more than is possible, not only in the political environment, but also within the economic constraints. By the way, Hillary Clinton knew that. She understands virtually everything about the policy specifics of every healthcare overhaul legislators have proposed in the past 25 years. I weep that she is not our president.

Next, Senator Sanders wants to get money out of politics. So do I. So did Secretary Clinton. Merrick Garland or any justice Hillary Clinton would have nominated would have accomplished that, would have overturned *Citizens United v. FEC*. Neil Gorsuch and any additional justices nominated by the Republican president will accomplish the reverse, legally enshrining corporate control of the political process.

In fact, I believe corporate money in our politics is among the biggest problems we face in the United States — although even bigger crises loom. For example, global climate change continues to destroy many of the planet's species. We are experiencing severe weather more frequently: tornadoes, hurricanes, and droughts leading to a dramatic increase in wildfires. Yet Republicans either don't believe the climate is changing or don't believe we should take any action to solve the problem. Sanders and Hillary Clinton both believe we should take dramatic action.

Here's another crisis: We could navigate an aircraft carrier through the gap separating the wealthy from the poor in our country. Hillary Clinton and Bernie Sanders believe we should fix that problem. They both believe we need stronger protections for unions. Both believe we need higher minimum wages. They both believe the federal government must support and pay for infrastructure improvements throughout the country. We need to fix our bridges. Doing so will put millions of people to work, and both Bernie Sanders and Hillary Clinton believe that.

There exists almost no daylight between the positions and beliefs held by Senator Sanders and Hillary Clinton. But Sanders, and perhaps you, his supporters, believed there was going to be a revolution, and once the people revolted, apparently all our other problems would have magically solved themselves. I wish I had that kind of optimism. I wish I could have seen an indication that he had some idea how to start that revolution. But I did not believe it then, and still do not believe it now.

You say you want a revolution? Well all right, we all wanna change the world.

I kept waiting for some sign the senator believed in this peaceful revolution he promised. Any non-violent change of power under our laws requires Congressional control. I waited in vain for Bernie Sanders to indicate he was supporting candidates for House and Senate seats. Not until he lost the nomination did he finally start helping other progressive politicians. The opportunity for a 2016 progressive revolution had passed.

❧

Now that Sanders has gained a national reputation and access to the bully pulpit, I am thrilled to see him campaigning for the same issues he has always held dear, the issues you and I hold dear. I would be more thrilled if he had remained in the Democratic Party. If he wants a revolution, he should be raising money for the DNC. Doing so would enable him to shape the Party. He could be raising money for Democrats in purple districts, especially those currently held by Republicans. He could use his high profile to help get people elected in state and local offices.

Bill Maher, who supported Sanders for president, interviewed him in February of 2016 and suggested he should begin educating the public about what socialism really means. Sanders disagreed, which floored me. I actually screamed at him through my television. For the record, I don't believe he heard me.

I think one of the biggest problems with his candidacy was the American electorate's misunderstanding regarding the meaning of socialism. They don't understand that public schools and Social Security are both socialist programs. If they believe we should have public police departments or Medicare, they're socialists. If they believe we should have public fire departments or publically constructed roads and bridges, they're socialists.

A supporter at a town hall asked Sanders whether an increase in minimum wage to $15 per hour would cause such massive inflation that the $15 per hour would yield no real benefits. His answer? The increase in minimum wage would grow the economy. According to some economists, he may be right. But he did not answer the question, so the supporter asked again, rephrasing. Senator Sanders responded that while there might be some small amount of inflation, what was important to remember is that the increase in minimum wage would grow the economy. This interchange also floored me.

His failure to answer the question was not what bothered me. That's typical politician stuff, right? What bothered me was that it didn't seem as though he could answer. In virtually every real-world example of minimum wage increase, little to zero inflation has resulted. When minimum wages increase, most of the higher cost to business owners and producers are borne by capitalists. In other words, the wealthiest make a little less so the poorest can make a little more. Business owners who choose to raise prices lose market share to businesses that leave prices unchanged. Prices for goods and services rarely increase when the working poor get a little raise. This is particularly true when all the poorest workers get raises simultaneously, such as happens when wages are increased by law. Furthermore, raising minimum wage will reduce the federal deficit. Almost every extra dollar paid to minimum wage earners by their employers would offset a dollar the federal government currently pays in the form of an Earned Income Tax Credit.

What annoyed me about the way Bernie Sanders responded to the question was that he did not appear to fully appreciate the dynamics of increasing minimum wages. Apparently, he embraces $15 per hour minimum wage because he believes in the ideology of helping people who are stuck earning the lowest wages. While helping low-wage earners is certainly a noble cause, any potentially negative outcomes did not figure into his analysis. History indicates such an increase in minimum wage will not cost jobs or lead to significant inflation, yet Sanders devoted no energy to those considerations.

We should be looking for leaders who have faith in their ideals but also consider the consequences of implementing their proposals, who are willing to work through details to be sure their proposals actually lead to the intended goals. Bernie Sanders is long on faith, but short on details. We need leaders who look for real underlying causes of problems instead of phony scapegoats like globalization. Reining in free trade would have a greater negative impact than any benefits we might anticipate. Technology, not globalization, has been the biggest job killer. Unions could help lift wages in the new economy, but many union members supported the Republican nominee in 2016. And why shouldn't they have abandoned Democrats? The Democratic party has delivered nothing to unions for decades.

Additionally, Bernie Sanders did not appear to understand that economically disadvantaged people, whether white, African American, Latino or any other stripe, need a fair shot at the best possible education from the moment they are born. He especially did not seem to understand the very revolution he sought requires far more than the presidency.

That explains why I switched allegiance to Hillary Clinton, but not why I am boring you with my opinions. Let me explain: Despite the fact that the two candidates agreed on nearly every policy goal, Senator Sanders kept insisting Hillary Clinton was corrupt and that the election was rigged. She was not corrupt, and the election certainly was not rigged in her favor, but Senator Sanders used those specific phrases repeatedly. Then the Republican nominee used them. They were extremely effective for him. They turned some of you into non-voters. His words and this election outcome have left many of you so disenchanted that you question whether democracy is even a good idea or worth all the trouble. Well, that is not okay with me. Democracy does matter, and the nation needs you.

As I canvassed for Hillary Clinton during the summer and autumn, I ran into dozens and dozens of twenty-somethings who told me they would not vote at all, or worse, they were planning to vote for the Republican. Nearly all of these people were first-time registered voters who had caucused for Sanders. When the general election came around, they were true to their word. Many of them voted Republican. We now know Russian cyber warriors deployed bots that directed 82% of the traffic from websites supporting Sanders to websites disseminating fake news about Hillary Clinton. Sanders softened you up with words about Clinton being corrupt and the election being rigged, then the Republican nominee and Russia used the Vermont Senator's words to deliver the final blow.

As it turned out, the Democratic National Committee may have unfairly favored Hillary Clinton's candidacy over that of Bernie Sanders. I write "may have" because I'm not sure it was unfair. Some emails showed two DNC workers plotting to help Hillary Clinton win the nomination. It is not clear from those emails whether the two workers ever acted on their inclinations. To the contrary, other emails illustrate that DNC Chairwoman Debbie Wasserman Schultz had chastised those workers for even discussing what could have been construed as political problems for Sanders.

And what had Sanders done for the Democratic party? He served as an unaffiliated legislator his entire public life, loyal to no political party. When he decided he would like to be president, he attempted to usurp the credibility of a party he previously shunned. Once Hillary Clinton had the nomination sewn up, Sanders promptly left the party.

Finally, Bill Maher was so right. Senator Sanders absolutely did need, and still needs to explain the meaning of socialism. Almost all of us, even most Republican voters, are socialists who refuse to face that truth. Most Republicans believe themselves to be Capitalists, which is nothing more than a religion in which the adherents revere Capital as their Almighty. Socialism is a similar religion, but its adherents revere a Social Contract. Some worshippers in both religions see the Free Market as one pathway to achieve their goals, but most Capitalists fail to recognize what they're actually worshipping: Money. The practice of money worship actually shuns free markets. Such worship cedes control to corporate Robots programmed to achieve only one goal: profit, sometimes at the expense of free markets, other times at the expense of protections for consumers, even at the expense of human life, if necessary. I know that seems wacky, so for a full explanation about Corporate Robots, please go back and read Chapter 2: *Mythical Conversation Among Liberals and Conservatives in Which Everyone Remains Respectful and Civil*, and Chapter 3: *The People v. Robots — Argument before the Supreme Court about Corporations*.

Meanwhile, socialists simply want a social contract that guarantees we all get some basic needs met, even if we were not lucky enough to be born with wealth. We think access to healthcare and education are rights everybody should have. Access to police and fire protection are rights we all should enjoy. Socialism is not a four-letter word. I hope Bernie Sanders will continue broadcasting that message.

Most of all, Bernie Bros, I hope you will reject the need for purity or perfection. Neither exists. For generations people have used the phrase "lesser of two evils" to explain their attitude toward the electoral process. Although that platitude helps people hold their noses while casting a vote, I hope you will reject the image. No politician, no relative, no friend, no spouse, will ever embody your idea of perfection. Face it, even you do not embody your own idea of perfection. So instead of seeking a purity you, yourself, are not capable of delivering, try supporting candidates who come closest to representing your ideals and also have a chance of winning. Your country needs you, so please, never sacrifice the good in pursuit of fictional perfection.

❧

11

Conversation with Elizabeth Warren

Why, oh why didn't you run for president in 2016? Sure, I liked Hillary Clinton, even campaigned for her. Knocked on over 300 doors while holding down a full-time job. But the country was yearning for a longtime progressive who had always stuck to her principles. Didn't you hear us begging?

"You didn't build that!" How I love that line! Please help your party find the next You — a woman with the same beliefs and similar knowledge base. Find someone who can start leading the party. Find someone who can begin preparing for the presidency. But, please, could you hurry? I cannot take much more of all this winning the president promised.

12

Conversation with the 45th President

"AMERICA, LOVE IT OR LEAVE IT!" You remember that old complaint, right? I'd be willing to bet a pizza dinner at the restaurant of your choice, anywhere in the world, that at least once in your mid-twenties you either uttered that phrase or were on the receiving end of it being shouted at you. One way or the other, I'm betting you've heard the words. Assuming that's true, I'd also guess you remember people used that platitude to make one point: Stop protesting. Stop whining about our country's participation in the Vietnam War. Stop agitating for women's equal rights. Stop protesting against violation of the rights of African Americans.

People marched to demand fair treatment of Latinos and Farm workers. They held sit-ins against the use of nuclear fuel for power plants and the poisoning of our atmosphere and waterways. They used legal action to continue fighting against segregation in public schools.

Lately, inspired by apparently hate-filled campaign rhetoric leading to your victory in the recent election, I've been thinking about moving away. That's why that old phrase has been on my mind. I was asking myself, what would be a valid reason for leaving my country of birth, the country I grew up loving? And the answer, on one level, is pretty simple. I would seriously consider leaving if I stopped loving it.

But leaving my country of birth would kind of mean I'm quitting. And it occurs to me, in a way, America is largely a nation of quitters. A majority of people living here, documented or not, all of us except Native Americans and most African Americans are either quitters or the descendants of quitters. We trace our ancestry to people who chose to leave their birthplace and embark on an experiment: Could they improve their lives by emigrating? And since we built a great nation, the most powerful in history, it logically follows that leaving our native countries worked out pretty well for most of us in this natural experiment called the United States of America. Obviously, many Native Americans argue the experiment didn't work out well for them. Some African Americans might echo that claim. They might point out how badly the experiment has failed them so far. I do not pretend to have any first-hand personal insight regarding the lives of African Americans, so if you wish to learn more about how some might be disposed toward the American experiment, I suggest reading *Between the World and Me* by Ta-Nehisi Coates. But for most people, coming to America turned out to be a great choice. So I want to explore the circumstances that would make it a good choice to leave the United States behind.

⚜

If people no longer love their country, should they leave, and in Tina Turner's words, "What's love got to do with it?" If I compare love of country to love for a spouse, I am forced to note that many people get divorced when they realize they no longer love their spouse. In Ms. Turner's case, that choice was closely associated with a life of being battered, so, not a surprising decision. You also made that choice a couple times. On the other hand, many people stay married despite no longer being in love, some, despite being beaten and raped. So what makes them stay, and is that a good decision?

Financial security often plays a big part in this decision, though you, Mr. President, probably find it difficult to identify with that particular problem. I think some people stay married because the alternative puts too much financial strain on both would-be former spouses. The cost of the divorce itself is high. The cost of maintaining two households instead of one can be ruinous. Many people, despite no longer loving each other, choose to stay married. With patience and, I assume, the right kind of counseling, that works out alright for some.

By the way, before we go further, I am exceedingly happily married, love my wife, and she's the best friend I've ever had — although no one understands what she sees in me. I also love my country, but a couple of things have changed. It is no longer the best place I've ever been, and I am less than exceedingly happy to be living here.

So I am seriously considering moving away. Divorcing my country, though, that would be costly. I've got fourteen years vested toward a retirement pension that I cannot start collecting unless I invest another six years. Prior to my current career, I had thirty years invested in a Social Security pension that will be reduced nearly 60% because of my years in teaching. In case you're doing the math, I started my first formal job at age 13. The point is, I'm sorta stuck. I may not be able to afford leaving America even if I decide I must. But this is not about me. I'm only using my own story as an example.

For the sake of the country, you want me to stay, you need me to stay. You say you have a great brain, and I believe that could be true. So believe this: I'm a great teacher. If I left, the United States of America would fill my teaching position so fast it would probably depress me a little. But what if a million of us left? What if the most experienced and dedicated among us were to leave? Not just teachers, but police officers, programmers, doctors, carpenters, actuaries: If a large swath of us left, would the country notice? You bet it would! Though the circumstances would be the reverse of John Galt's role in *Atlas, Shrugged* by Ayn Rand, I believe the economy would truly grind to a halt. On the other hand, if the world's real corporate leaders led a Galt-like strike, new leaders would take their places so fast it would make our collective heads spin. Take your job, for example: If you decided to leave, we already know Mike Pence would fill your shoes instantaneously.

I am not the only citizen thinking about leaving, believe me. On election night, Americans crashed the Canadian government's immigration website.[1] The site couldn't handle the traffic from across the border. The next day, Google search terms related to "moving to Canada" spiked by 1,174%. That's why I'm trying to figure out if all these anxious citizens moving away from the United States would be making a good choice. Thinking about why people moved here in the first place might be the right place to start this analysis.

❦

The settlers of Jamestown in present day Virginia, the first people known to have survived the ordeal of establishing a British Colony in the New World, were sent primarily to exploit economic opportunities for their financiers. Many were expecting to find precious metals such as gold, silver, and copper.[2] In 1609, they found, instead, famine and disease to such a large extent that they resorted to cannibalism to survive.[3] Most members of the Plymouth Colony established in Massachusetts in 1620 also immigrated looking for economic opportunity.

Another 40 percent of Plymouth's first wave of colonists had come seeking a place where they could practice Christianity their way without being persecuted as they had been in England: The Pilgrims. The democratic setup and free exercise of religion in Plymouth influenced politics in England and the Colonies. Connecticut, Rhode Island, New

Jersey, and Pennsylvania incorporated guarantees of religious freedom into their Colonial constitutions. Each of these four colonies became a refuge for persecuted religious minorities, and continued to be safe havens after the Founders signed the Declaration of Independence in 1776 and after they agreed upon a governing body of laws in 1777.

When those laws, the Articles of Confederation, failed to adequately serve the country's needs, the Framers met for the Constitutional Convention in Philadelphia in 1787 to improve the Articles of Confederation. By the end of the first day, they had agreed the Articles could not be made to work. So they began crafting a fresh document. After four months of negotiations, they had written and agreed upon the new United States Constitution with its seven articles.

Two years later Congress sent a Bill of Rights containing twelve amendments to each state for approval. Ten of those twelve amendments were approved by December of 1791. The First Amendment ratified begins: "Congress shall make no law respecting an establishment of religion, or prohibiting the free exercise thereof..." It took 171 years, but the tradition established by The Pilgrims in Plymouth Colony became embodied in our Constitution and has remained unchanged ever since.

⚬⚬⚬

In pursuit of the religious freedom guaranteed by our Constitution, people have been immigrating to the United States for more than two centuries. My family came here partially for that reason. Although Hitler did everything he could to exterminate all the world's Jews, by no means did he invent anti-Semitism. In the late 1800's, two of my grandparents and all my great-grandparents fled the rampant persecution of Jews in Eastern Europe. They put down roots in Colorado. They became successful real estate developers and built and owned hotels, apartments and banks. They built vacation resort condominiums in Vail, Dillon and Frisco, Colorado. Sounds somewhat familiar, right? Not all my family history parallels yours, though. No one in my family has ever dodged military service.

My family, like millions of others, came here for religious freedom, then participated in making America wealthy. But it's not the wealth that made America great. It's the religious freedom, the rights to privacy, to due process of laws, and to be tried by a jury of our peers. And yes, greatness does spring from the right to participate in all aspects of the economy regardless of race, religion, color, creed, or gender. Those are the ideals that make America great. Money? Getting rich? Man, it's just money. It's not worthy of worship. But of course, if that is your preferred religion, in this country you are free to believe as you wish.

Many people immigrated to the United States fleeing religious and ethnic persecution and poverty. Others fled military conscription. Regardless of their reasons for coming to America, most eventually were able to find prosperity — if they were white and European. Which leads me to the real reason I love the United States of America — not for the reality brought to fruition by the Framers of the Constitution in 1787, but for the greatness realized because of human struggles throughout the ensuing 190 years. I love this country for the ideals set forth in the Declaration of Independence, even though many of those principles had to wait two centuries before being codified into our laws.

Instead of honoring the Declaration, the Framers wrote a constitution that guaranteed the continuing right to own slaves for a score of years. Their Constitution limited suffrage to property-owning white men. Those limitations are not cited in the Constitution directly. They were embodied in our law via the right reserved unto states to define their own voting procedures.

Nevertheless, by 1856 every state had extended suffrage to all free white male citizens, even those who did not own property. Then the Civil War and the 13th, 14th and 15th Amendments extended freedom and citizenship to former slaves. If they were men, they also received the right to vote, though most Southern states limited those rights through literacy tests and poll taxes, not to mention intimidation, overt violence, lynchings, and other terrorist tactics.

In the late 1880's Indians who renounced tribal affiliations received suffrage, and in 1919 Indians who had served in the military during World War I were granted citizenship and suffrage. A year later, women received the right to vote. People of Japanese ancestry born on U.S. soil gained citizenship and suffrage in 1952 with passage of the McCarran-Walter Act. In 1965, the Voting Rights Act passed, protecting suffrage for African Americans and Latinos. Finally, 18-year olds got the right to vote in 1971, a result of complaints that the average age of U.S. soldiers conscripted to fight and die in Vietnam was only nineteen.

Honestly, Mr. President, you have every reason to be proud of your election. Even though you lost to Hillary Clinton by nearly 3 million votes, you received votes from almost 20% of the U.S. population. By contrast, George Washington, who ran unopposed and received 100% of the available votes, even he was elected by only 6% of the population in 1788. So you might say you are more popular today than George Washington was in his own time. In fact, once you read that, I fully expect you to tweet it.

꧁꧂

But in case you missed it, the reason I love our country is because of the way it has evolved. I am supremely proud that we do have a country in which all people are endowed by our laws with equal access to unalienable rights to life, liberty, and the pursuit of happiness, as well as equal suffrage. I have been proud of the United States all my life even though it took 200 years for us to fully embrace the ideals set forth in the Declaration of Independence and echoed by President Abraham Lincoln at Gettysburg. I have been proud of my uncle, my father, and all who served with them in the

U.S. military to defeat Imperial Japan and Nazi Germany and help end the Holocaust.

I was especially proud when our country elected Barack Obama as its 44th president. When the Democratic Party nominated him, I was sure he would lose the general election, sure our country still harbored too much racism. I doubted we would elect a man who was half African American and raised by an atheist mother who had married a Kenyan man three months after becoming pregnant with their son. I have never been so happy to be wrong. Did his election make me believe racism in America was dead? Hell no! But it gave me hope that racism was fading, a creature of older generations, my generation and yours.

Then you started making a political name for yourself by claiming you had "people" investigating whether President Obama had been born in the United States. You implied he was not, and that he was a Muslim bent on harboring terrorists. I watched as you announced your candidacy with these racists comments in June of 2015: "When Mexico sends its people, they're not sending their best....They're sending people that have lots of problems... They're bringing drugs. They're bringing crime. They're rapists, and some, I assume, are good people."

Then you got elected. That's when I became ashamed of our country. You, Mr. President, are the biggest embarrassment our country has ever suffered. The fault is not all or even mostly yours. The fault lies with the electorate. Nearly 63 million people voted for you despite your innumerable lies, your appeals to racism, your unjustifiable fear mongering and your religious bigotry. My shame springs from the massive number of Americans who were willing to vote for your presidency.

I feel shame that you wasted no time before rewarding those voters for their hatred. You immediately signed that executive order to ban Muslims. Yes I know the order was not titled a Muslim ban, nor did it contain the phrase Muslim ban. But you know something? The Constitution never contained the words *slave* or *slavery*, nevertheless, Article I, Section 2 still managed to count each slave as three-fifths of a person. Similarly, your administration has now managed to introduce a second Muslim ban, again, without using the phrase Muslim ban. Sure, I oppose your agenda, but it's your 63 million supporters who make me feel shame.

Many still support your presidency in spite of, or because of, your appointment of white supremacist Steve Bannon to be your top advisor. They admire your choice of known racist Jeff Sessions for U.S. Attorney General. You appoint Ben Carson and Betsy DeVos to cabinet positions they know nothing about. You think it is okay to, "Grab 'em by the pussy!" You appoint Michael Flynn to be your National Security Advisor, an officer who President Obama fired for incompetence. You appoint Rick Perry to head the department of "Oops." To lead the Department of Commerce, you appoint your friend Wilbur Ross, a man with a large stake in a Cypriot bank that launders money for Russian kleptocrats. You falsely claim the real unemployment rate is 42%.[4] You tweet the lie: "How low has President Obama gone to tapp (sic) my phones..."[5] You falsely state: "The concept of global warming was created by and for the Chinese in order to make U.S. manufacturing non-competitive."[6] You claim crime rates have risen for decades, when they are barely above unprecedented lows.[7] You claim undocumented immigrants commit more crime than citizens, which belies statistical evidence.[8]

You cling to the claim of a connection between vaccines and autism despite two decades of scientific debunking. In a 2015 debate you stated, "Autism has become an epidemic." That claim is demonstrably false. You said, "I'm totally in favor of vaccines, but I want smaller doses over a longer period of time." Science proves such a schedule puts the population at risk for several epidemics that could cause mass fatalities. Then you babbled, "People that work for me, just the other day, two years old, two and a half years old, a child, a beautiful child went to have the vaccine and came back and a week later, got a tremendous fever, got very, very sick, now is autistic."[9] The only part of that sentence at all plausible is that you put a two-year-old toddler to work for you.

You claim every real news medium is fake and all fake news outlets are real. Are you incapable of saying or tweeting anything true? Are you unable to distinguish your own fictions from truth? Can you make your case and win support without relying on the electorate's ignorance? Have you absolutely no faith in the human capacity to come to a conclusion that you should be supported for your policy positions based on their merits, rather than your lies and nonsense? Or do you simply have no agenda for the country, only an agenda to advance what's good for you?

Let's proceed on the assumption that such a cynical appraisal is completely unfair and inaccurate. Instead, I'm going to assume you spent $68,000 on a treasonous exploratory business venture in Cuba[10] because you think of laws as more like guidelines, really, for other people to follow — people who aren't rich. Perhaps you made an honest mistake when you spent your non-profit foundation's money to settle your personal lawsuits. When you used that foundation's money to contribute to Pam Bondi's campaign for Attorney General of Florida, maybe that had no connection to her office ending its investigation into whether your unaccredited university had defrauded students out of tens of millions of dollars.[11] Maybe you really are completely innocent, kind, smart, and important.

I'll assume you ran for president of the United States because you believed you had some really good ideas that nobody else was able to think of. After all, you have "a really good brain" and according to you, our leaders are "stupid, stupid people."[12] During your campaign, you criticized President George W. Bush for his policy in Iraq, Marco

Rubio for his voting record, John McCain for his war record, and John Kasich for his eating habits.

$$\sim\!\!\sim\!\!\sim$$

Cannot help but notice, now that you achieved your initial goal, now that you are president, you seem to be executing the Republican agenda of the past four decades. The Muslim ban? Deporting undocumented Mexicans? Mistrust of everyone not white enough? Republicans have been blowing those dog whistles since before you were born. The only difference is you're using a train whistle. We hear you loud and clear. Tax cuts for corporations and the extremely wealthy? It's been 36 years since I met a Republican who wouldn't applaud that. Dismantle the social safety net: Social Security, Medicare, Obama Care, Medicaid? Republicans opposed each of those measures from the moment they were proposed, and they began working toward their demise the moment each became law.

Most of your proposals are simply vulgar repackaging of the worst ideas ever put forward by the Republican Party. Your other notions obviously please Russian President Vladimir Putin. Nothing could make him happier than splitting apart long-honored alliances among all his international adversaries. He wants us to browbeat member nations of the North Atlantic Treaty Organization, crush international trade, and abandon the Trans Pacific Partnership.

By ending negotiations on TPP, you probably made Xi Jinping pretty happy too. But let's get back to Putin. He was pleased to see you embrace Nigel Farage and Brexit. He would love to hear you endorse Marine Le Pen next time she runs for President of France and Frauke Petry for German Chancellor. All those ideas are cyber war policies of Russia, so yes, Putin must be satisfied that his project is working as planned.

$$\sim\!\!\sim\!\!\sim$$

Proceeding on the assumption that you do have the best interests of the United States of America at heart, I would like you to accept the likelihood that Vladimir Putin is not our friend. Furthermore, I hope you will consider the possibility that the Republican Party might have been wrong about economics ever since trickle down became a phrase people take seriously. Imagine that the best-educated, best-trained scientists in the world are right about anthropogenic climate change and Republican politicians are wrong. Think for just a moment that your new National Security Advisor, General H.R. McMasters is right while your gut and Steve Bannon are wrong about the consequences of using the phrase Radical Islamic Terrorists.

Finally, please understand your stay in the White House is at our pleasure and your work as president is temporary. You do not own the job; it owns you. We do not serve to gratify your needs; you serve to gratify ours. We are under no obligation to show you any loyalty; your obligation is to remain loyal to us and the Constitution. When your term is up, We the People would be grateful if the job still commanded the world's respect when it is taken over by the next employee we hire.

No animals were harmed while these two
photographs were composited into one.

13

Conversation with the Democratic Party

Calling all Democrats lost in the wilderness! I am talking about Democrats living in political districts so gerrymandered that only Republican candidates have any hope of winning in the foreseeable future. When it has become impossible to beat them, join them. Register Republican. Find a few extreme right-wingers to run against your current representative, people who can split their vote among several candidates. Then find a liberal Republican to run against them all.

No such thing as a liberal Republican in your district? Become one yourself. Run for office. Think judo. Employ the power of the Grand Old Party's extremism against itself. Split the votes among their extremists in primaries, and allow the liberal to emerge victorious. Anyway, that's one idea. Maybe it could work.

৩৽৵

14

Conversation with Republican-Leaning Libertarians

P resuming I understand correctly, the *liberta-* in your moniker stands for freedom. You want small government so you can be free from interference in your lives. Great idea! I completely agree, but my philosophy goes further. I also want corporations to be small so I can be free from their interference in my life. Corporations must be carefully regulated so humans and all other life on Earth can be free from the air, water, and mind pollution they spew in their relentless pursuit of profit. Corporations are tasked with representing shareholders and increasing their profits, even when that results in harming, maiming, or killing humans.

Government's task is to represent the greater good of all the country's people. The United States began as a nation whose Founders distrusted power being concentrated in too few hands. Thus the Constitution created a body of laws separating authority among Legislative, Executive, and Judicial branches, among national, state, and local governments, and among the people themselves. Although the country began as a flawed nation in which only a few privileged people had the right to vote, one by one, new groups gained suffrage — men without property, former male slaves, native-American men, women, Asians, and finally, young people. The United States has never been the nation it should be, but it usually has been heading in the right direction.

Certainly the country has taken some wrong turns — the Civil War, for example. But even the Civil War is evidence the nation was stumbling toward a better road than the path of slavery it left behind. Soon afterward, however, the country faced a growing problem. Enormous power had accumulated in the hands of a few wealthy family trusts, corporations that had gained monopoly control over industries such as oil, banking, and railroads. These trusts used their power and influence to destroy competition and exploit consumers and workers, proving the Founders had been justified in their fears regarding too much power in the hands of too few people.

Only government could provide a check against the growing power of trusts, stifle their influence, and restore protections for people. In a 1911 Supreme Court decision forcing the breakup of Standard Oil Company, Justice John Marshall Harlan noted the downcast mood of the country twenty years earlier that had led to new legislative action. To paraphrase:

> Everywhere in 1890 was a deep feeling of unrest. The nation had been rid of human slavery, but the conviction was universal that the country was in real danger from another kind of slavery that would result from aggregations of capital in the hands of a few individuals and corporations. These were controlling, exclusively for their own profit, the entire business of the country, including the production and sale of the necessities of life. Everyone felt this danger must be met firmly by regulations that would adequately protect the people against oppression. Congress, under authority granted by the Constitution, could regulate interstate commerce. That authority is

paramount, devised by the Framers to protect the essential rights of life, liberty, and property.

Guided by the goal that people should not be dominated by vast monopolies exercising power to advance their own selfish ends with disregard to the general welfare, Congress passed the Sherman Antitrust Act of 1890.[1]

Thus the nation began returning volleys in a war between monopolies and the government of, by, and for the people. Breaking up the largest trust, Standard Oil, took more than twenty years and required a determined President Theodore Roosevelt with help from one of the first investigative reporters, Ida Tarbell. Her series of articles in McClure's Magazine exposed collusion among John D. Rockefeller and several railroad magnates. Together, they skirted laws by manipulating freight charges to help Standard Oil destroy and take over its competition, all to increase profit by raising prices on consumers.[2] After the 1911 Supreme Court decision, Standard Oil split into 34 separate companies.

Amid the Great Depression, Franklin D. Roosevelt renewed the battle, signing the 1933 Banking Act to protect consumers. This Act restored consumer faith in banks by establishing government-guaranteed insurance for depositors. Also, provisions of the Act known as Glass-Steagall prevented banks from taking excessive risks and from engaging in securities brokerage activities.[3] Banks had loaned money for investments in the stock market, providing up to 90% of the purchase price. When stock prices declined dramatically throughout the summer of 1929, banks demanded payment, but selling the stock did not give borrowers enough money to repay their loans. Selling stock en masse pushed prices lower, forcing banks to demand payment on more loans. This created a feedback loop ending with the October 1929 Stock Market Crash and the collapse of 9,000 banks. Glass-Steagall stabilized banks for the first time ever, providing a foundation for an expanding economy.

Throughout the 1930's, a series of federal labor laws gave another economic boost. The National Labor Relations Act of 1935 protected workers' rights to organize and collectively bargain with their employers.[4] Also passed in 1935, the Social Security Act guaranteed income to retired people over 65 years old. The Walsh-Healey Public Contracts Act of 1936[5] and The Fair Labor Standards Act of 1938 established overtime pay and minimum wages, and prohibited employment of youths under 16 years of age.[6] These laws put money directly into the pockets of the newly rooted Middle Class.

In the following decade, the federal government provided arguably the biggest boost ever to the Middle Class by passing the Servicemen's Readjustment Act of 1944. It gave returning veterans of World War II a free ride to college. Better known as the G.I. Bill, it paid for their tuition and textbooks, and gave them a monthly stipend. Alternatively, veterans could collect up to one year of unemployment compensation while they looked for work. Again, this put money in the pockets of the burgeoning Middle Class. It also gave the United States the best educated work force the country had ever known.

During the 1950's, 60's and 70's, a combination of Supreme Court decisions and Congressional actions spurred by non-violent protests provided legal protections for racial minorities. With movement toward equality in education, equal employment, fair housing, and access to the voting booth, African Americans and Latinos finally began getting a chance to join the growing Middle Class.

This succession of policies boosted the quality of life for ordinary people by safeguarding their bank deposits, their health, their earning power, their value to employers, and their retirement income. In turn, ordinary folks created new jobs by consuming. As their consumption increased, more people found jobs meeting the greater demand for goods and services.

Consequently, the economy grew rapidly, which provided benefits for people far outside the Middle Class. Nearly everyone profited. Almost everyone's wealth increased as the wealth of the Middle Class grew. Though some people remained in poverty, none of the super-wealthy suffered from the rise of Middle Class America.

But in 1981 our nation took a wrong turn. Collectively, we decided government could not be trusted. We turned, instead, to Robots and placed our trust with them. At the urging of corporate lobbyists, state governments have dismantled worker and union protections, leading to declining wages, relatively speaking, and the fall of the Middle Class. At the urging of bank industry lobbyists, Congress dismantled Glass-Steagall, leading directly to three major industry-wide failures, and the decline of the Middle Class. The most recent failure, that of 2007-2008, nearly collapsed the whole world's banking system and economy. Now, at the urging of energy industry lobbyists, the 45th president is dismantling environmental protections, withdrawing our nation from the Paris Climate Accord while routinely denying the existence of global warming caused by human activity.

Libertarians, the United States system of government is tasked with representing humans. One of its main jobs is to protect us from the ravages corporations would leave in their wake if they were left to operate as they pleased. We need government to interfere on our behalf. The alternative is to lose all our freedom to corporate Robots who care nothing for us at all.

⌘

FOR THE RECORD, Libertarians, this is the least amount of oversight I can imagine coming from government in order to adequately protect our democracy —

For Earth:
- Protect the climate.
- Stop subsidizing carbon energy. Instead, levy a planet-restoration tax on carbon emissions.
- Protect rivers and oceans.

For truth:

- Reinstate the Fairness Doctrine and apply it to all electronic media: broadcast, cable, radio, and internet.
- Require speakers in every forum to identify themselves. Ban anonymous donations, anonymous campaigns, anonymous advertisements, anonymous internet posts, and all posts, tweets or "likes" by bots.
- Ban political speech of non-human entities such as for-profit corporations.

For civil rights:

- Protect women's rights to equal pay and equal opportunity in the workforce and in housing.
- Protect a woman's right to choose.
- Protect the equal rights of whites, blacks, native Americans, Latinos, Asians, and so on.
- Recognize that Black Lives Matter too.
- Protect religious freedoms of Catholics, Shiites, Jews, Protestants, Sikhs, Hindus, Atheists, Presbyterians, Animists, Sunnis, Mormons, Agnostics, Methodists, Buddhists, and so on.
- Protect the rights of people who are lesbian, gay, bisexual, transgender, queer, or heterosexual.

For the Middle Class and the economy in general:

- Protect unions.
- Ban so-called Right to Work laws at state and federal levels.
- Protect collective bargaining rights.
- Protect workers by raising minimum wage to bring all full-time workers out of poverty and instituting automatic increases pegged to inflation.
- Give work documents, but not citizenship, to immigrants whose children are citizens.
- Close our borders with intelligent surveillance, not a wall.

- Give addicts of all ethnicities medical help, not prison sentences.
- Charge a fee for every securities transaction initiated by a computer or Artificial Intelligence.
- Require securities brokers to act as fiduciaries for their clients.
- Tax capital gains at the same rate as ordinary income.
- Treat hedge-fund management "gains" as ordinary income.
- Regulate banks and all other financial institutions by strengthening Dodd-Frank. Recognize insurance policies are a form of deposit in need of consumer protections. Require all financial institutions to keep at least 10% of its "deposits" in reserve. Separate banks and insurance companies from securities brokers as was the case under Glass-Steagall.
- Enforce anti-trust laws, thereby promoting free trade and commerce by recognizing that corporations seek to restrict competition.
- Recognize that every human will need health care eventually, so government should be the single payer — Medicare for All. No Robot should ever be allowed to profit from insuring our access to health care.
- Guarantee integration and equal education in public schools.
- Pay only for public schools — no vouchers allowed for private school funding.
- Ban for-profit charter schools funded with public money.
- Guarantee paid family leave for at least three months upon the arrival of newborns.

For fair access to government and to restore the public's confidence in representation, pass Constitutional amendments to implement the following protections to the electoral process:
- Eliminate voter identification laws.
- Institute vote by mail in every state.
- Eliminate the Electoral College and replace it with a popular vote for president.

- Institute non-partisan federal government oversight of redistricting in states.
- Institute a presidential electoral system featuring a final runoff election between the two recipients of the greatest number of votes if neither won a majority in the initial election.
- Institute federal government oversight of elections.

THE END

Notes

Chapter 1
Henry Blodget. (10-15-2011). Amazing chart shows 90% of the country has gotten shafted over the past 30 years. Business Insider. Retrieved 5-2-2017 from http://www.businessinsider.com/income-inequality-charts-2011-10
2 The state of working America. Economic Policy Institute. Retrieved 5-2-2017 from http://stateofworkingamerica.org/who-gains/#/?start=2001&end=2008
3 Edwin Rios and Dave Gilson. (12-22-2016). 11 charts that show income inequality isn't getting better anytime soon. Mother Jones. Retrieved 5-2-2017 from http://www.motherjones.com/politics/2016/12/america-income-inequality-wealth-net-worth-charts
4 Walter Quattrociocchi. (April, 2017). Inside the echo chamber. Scientific American. Pages 61-63.
5 Daniel Ellsberg. (7-4-2013). Democracy Now! Retrieved 6-16-2017 from https://www.democracynow.org/2013/7/4/how_the_pentagon_papers_came_to
6 Bob Woodward. (2005). The secret man. New York City: Simon and Shuster. Page 107.
7 Bob Woodward and Carl Bernstein. (1974). All the president's men. New York City: Simon and Shuster. Pages 75-79.
8 Ibid. Pages 79-86.
9 David Folkenflik. (10-19-2013). The birth of Fox News. Salon. Retrieved 6-15-2017 from http://www.salon.com/2013/10/19/the_birth_of_fox_news/
10 Project Steve. Frequently asked questions. Retrieved 6-11-2017 from https://ncse.com/project-steve-faq
11 Craig Welch. (3-2-2015). Climate change helped spark Syrian conflict, study says. National Geographic. Retrieved 5-2-2017 from http://news.nationalgeographic.com/news/2015/03/150302-syria-war-climate-change-drought/

Chapter 2
Caroline Scott. (5-2-2015). The forgotten victims. The Times. London. Retrieved 5-27-2017 from https://www.thetimes.co.uk/article/the-forgotten-victims-3pk3bf0fvw7
2 Jeffrey Wigand. (2000). Testimony of the 7 CEOs of big tobacco. Jeffrey Wigand.com. Retrieved 5-17-2017 from http://www.jeffreywigand.com/7ceos.php
3 U.S. Department of Health and Human Services. The Health Consequences of Smoking—50 Years of Progress A Report of the Surgeon General. Page 677. Retrieved 5-17-2017 from https://www.surgeongeneral.gov/library/reports/50-years-of-progress/full-report.pdf
4 Action on Smoking & Health. Tobacco statistics and health. Retrieved 5-17-2017 from http://ash.org/resources/tobacco-statistics-facts/

5 Centers for Disease Control and Prevention. Health effects. Smoking and tobacco Use. Retrieved 5-17-2017 from https://www.cdc.gov/tobacco/basic_information/health_effects/index.htm?gclid=Cj wKEAjw6e_IBRDvorfv2Ku79jMSJAAuiv9YVlsVdrAGtI987KQaeQDv5rxXnCbYbtVu MVVjtj6AXxoCgYPw_wcB

6 George Rennie. (7-7-2015). How big tobacco gifted campaigns of misdirection and misinformation to the gun lobby. The Conversation. Retrieved 5-17-2017 from http://theconversation.com/how-big-tobacco-gifted-campaigns-of-misdirection-and-misinformation-to-the-gun-lobby-45108

7 Howard Kurtz. (11-10-1995). 60 Minutes kills piece on tobacco industry. Washington Post. Retrieved 5-17-2017 from https://www.washingtonpost.com/archive/politics/1995/11/10/60-minutes-kills-piece-on-tobacco-industry/e8edb45c-57f4-4f34-9d7f-3b25db60b2d6/?utm_term=.d8e250b778cc

8 Benjamin Hulac. (7-20-2016). Same researchers to sway public: As early as the 1950s, the groups shared scientists and publicists to downplay dangers of smoking and climate change. Scientific American. Retrieved 5-19-2017 from https://www.scientificamerican.com/article/tobacco-and-oil-industries-used-same-researchers-to-sway-public1/

9 Leslie Stahl. (2-19-2017). Popular Remington 700 rifle linked to potentially deadly defect. 60 Minutes. Retrieved 5-19-2017 from http://www.cbsnews.com/news/popular-remington-700-rifle-linked-to-potentially-deadly-defects/

10 E.S. Grush; C.S. Saundy. Fatalities associated with crash induced fuel leakage and Fires. Ford Environmental and Safety Engineering. Retrieved 5-19-2017 from http://www.autosafety.org/wp-content/uploads/import/phpq3mJ7F_FordMemo.pdf

11 Jess Paul. (4-30-2017). Deadly explosion is a faint memory in state's history. The Denver Post - Denver & the West, Page 1B.

12 Colorado coalfield war project. A history of the Colorado coalfield war. Retrieved 5-14-2017 from http://www.du.edu/ludlow/cfhist3.html

13 William Dalrymple. (3-4-2015). The East India Company: The original corporate raiders. The Guardian. Retrieved 6-26-2017 from https://www.theguardian.com/world/2015/mar/04/east-india-company-original-corporate-raiders

Chapter 3

Stephen Bainbridge. (5-5-1912). Case law on the fiduciary duty of directors to maximize the wealth of corporate shareholders. ProfessorBainbridge.com. Retrieved 4-29-17 from http://www.professorbainbridge.com/professorbainbridgecom/2012/05/case-law-on-the-fiduciary-duty-of-directors-to-maximize-the-wealth-of-corporate-shareholders.html#_ftn3

2 Dodge v. Ford Motor Co. (1919). Retrieved 4-29-17 from https://pages.law.illinois.edu/aviram/Dodge.pdf

3 Judith Lichtenberg. (10-19-2010). Is pure altruism possible? The New York Times. Retrieved 4-29-2017 from https://opinionator.blogs.nytimes.com/2010/10/19/is-pure-altruism-possible/?_r=0

4 Valerio Capraro. (4-28-2015). The emergence of hyper-altruistic behaviour in conflictual situations. Retrieved 4-29-2017 from https://www.nature.com/articles/srep09916

5 Robert L. Pitman, et al. (7-20-2016). Humpback whales interfering when mammal-eating killer whales attack other species: Mobbing behavior and interspecific altruism? Marine Mammal Science. Retrieved 4-29-2017 from http://onlinelibrary.wiley.com/doi/10.1111/mms.12343/full

6 Press Associates, Inc. (4-29-2016). GOP bill overturns Labor Dept. restriction on financial advisers; Obama promises veto. Retrieved 5-27-2017 from http://www.peoplesworld.org/article/gop-bill-overturns-labor-dept-restriction-on-financial-advisers-obama-promises-veto/

7 Opensecrets.org. Clients lobbying on H.J.Res.88: Disapproving the rule submitted by the Department of Labor relating to the definition of the term "Fiduciary". Retrieved 5-27-2017 from https://www.opensecrets.org/lobby/billsum.php?id=hjres88-114

8 Barack Obama. Veto message from the president. White House office of the press secretary. Retrieved 5-27-2017 from https://static.votesmart.org/static/vetotext/56829.pdf

9 Mark Schoeff, Jr. (2-21-2017). Campaign spending up among advice groups. Investment News. Retrieved 5-27-2017 from http://www.investmentnews.com/article/20170221/FREE/170229987/campaign-spending-up-among-advice-groups

10 Jamie Hopkins. (2-3-2017). Trump signs memorandum shelving fiduciary standard for financial advisors. Forbes: Personal Finance. Retrieved 5-27-2017 from https://www.forbes.com/sites/jamiehopkins/2017/02/03/trump-signs-executive-order-shelving-fiduciary-standard-for-financial-advisors/#43c6d7f75863

11 Peter Overby. (1-20-2015). 5 years after Citizens United, secret money floods into U.S. politics. NPR. Retrieved 6-25-2017 from http://www.npr.org/2015/01/20/378525627/5-years-after-citizens-united-ruling-secret-money-floods-into-u-s-politics

12 John Cook. (9-30-2012). What happened to climate change? Fox News and the US elections. The Conversation. Retrieved 6-19-2017 from https://theconversation.com/what-happened-to-climate-change-fox-news-and-the-us-elections-9814

13 American Biome Institute. (1-20-2016). How many bacteria vs human cells are in the body? Retrieved 6-19-2017 from http://www.microbiomeinstitute.org/blog/2016/1/20/how-many-bacterial-vs-human-cells-are-in-the-body

14 Blodget, Amazing chart.

15 Buckley v. Valeo. (1-30-1976). Legal Information Institute. Cornell Law School. Retrieved 6-24-2017 from https://www.law.cornell.edu/supremecourt/text/424/1

16 Ibid.

17 Jacob Pramuk. (4-19-2017). Trump's inaugural committee raised a record $106.7 million -- here's who donated. CNBC. Retrieved 6-25-2017 from http://www.cnbc.com/2017/04/19/trumps-inaugural-committee-raised-a-record-106-7-million--heres-who-donated.html

18 University of Illinois. (12-16-2016). American Newspapers 1800 - 1860: City Papers. Retrieved 6-24-2017 from http://guides.library.illinois.edu/c.php?g=347656&p=2348306

[19] Ibid.
[20] Stanley Lebergott. (1960). Trends in the American Economy in the Nineteenth Century. The Conference on Research in Income and Wealth. National Bureau of Economic Research. Princeton University Press. Page 451. Retrieved 6-24-2017 from http://www.nber.org/chapters/c2486.pdf
[21] University of Illinois. American Newspapers.
[22] Ibid.

Chapter 4

W.W. Norton. On The End of Faith. Sam Harris website. Retrieved 5-7-2017 from https://www.samharris.org/books/the-end-of-faith
[2] Bill Maher. (10-6-14). Real Time with Bill Maher. HBO. Retrieved 2-19-17 from https://www.youtube.com/watch?v=vln9D81eO60
[3] This American Life. (10-28-2016). Will I know Anyone at This Party? Retrieved 2-19-17 from https://www.thisamericanlife.org/radio-archives/episode/600/transcript
[4] Ibid.
[5] National Report. Disclaimer. Retrieved 2-19-17 from http://nationalreport.net/disclaimer/
[6] Sam Harris. (10-6-14). Real Time with Bill Maher. HBO. Retrieved 2-20-17 from https://www.youtube.com/watch?v=vln9D81eO60
[7] Debbie Bryce. (6-5-14). "Center recognizes nine hate groups in Idaho." Idaho State Journal. Retrieved 2-20-17 from http://idahostatejournal.com/members/center-recognizes-nine-hate-groups-in-idaho/article_2fc18774-ec87-11e3-a505-001a4bcf887a.html; and Seaborn Larson. (2-15-17). "Hate groups on the rise across Montana, nation." Great Falls Tribune. Retrieved 2-20-17 from http://www.greatfallstribune.com/story/news/local/2017/02/15/hate-groups-rise-across-montana-nation/97970738/
[8] "Terrorism 2002-2005." U.S. Department of Justice: Federal Bureau of Investigations. Retrieved 2-20-17 from https://www.fbi.gov/stats-services/publications/terrorism-2002-2005
[9] "Saudi Arabia to lead Muslim coalition against terrorism." (12-15-15). The Jerusalem Post. Retrieved 2-20-2017 from http://www.jpost.com/Middle-East/Saudi-Arabia-to-lead-Muslim-coalition-against-terrorism-437341
[10] Michael Hirsh. (3-24-16). "Inside the FBI's secret Muslim network." Politico Magazine. Retrieved 2-20-2017 from http://www.politico.com/magazine/story/2016/03/fbi-muslim-outreach-terrorism-213765
[11] Emily Feldman. (12-9-15). "How Muslim groups, scholars have been fighting ISIS." NBC New York. Retrieved 2-20-17 from http://www.nbcnewyork.com/news/national-international/Muslim-Scholars-Groups-Against-ISIS-Speal-Out-361309791.html?fb_comment_id=958929974187115_1095607950519316#f2d02bf1b83ecc4
[12] Julie E. Ainsley; Dustin Volz; and Kristina Cooke. "Exclusive: Trump to focus counter-extremism program solely on Islam - sources." Reuters. Retrieved 2-20-27 from http://www.reuters.com/article/us-usa-trump-extremists-program-exclusiv-idUSKBN15G5VO

[13] Eitan Hersh. (6-28-16). "How many Republicans marry Democrats?" FiveThirtyEight. Retrieved 2-20-17 from https://fivethirtyeight.com/features/how-many-republicans-marry-democrats/

[14] Ben Mathis-Lilley. (1-31-17). First Muslim ban poll finds Americans support Trump order by 7-point margin. The Slate.com. Retrieved 4-28-17 from http://www.slate.com/blogs/the_slatest/2017/01/31/reuters_ipsos_muslim_ban_poll_finds_support_for_order.html

[15] Uri Friedman. "Where America's Terrorists Actually Come From." Atlantic. Retrieved. 2-20-17 from https://www.theatlantic.com/international/archive/2017/01/trump-immigration-ban-terrorism/514361/

[16] Jens M. Krogstad; Jeffrey S. Passel; and D'vera Cohen. (11-3-16). "5 facts about illegal immigration in the U.S." Fact Tank. Pew Research Center. Retrieved 2-20-17 from http://www.pewresearch.org/fact-tank/2016/11/03/5-facts-about-illegal-immigration-in-the-u-s/; and Ana Gonzalez-Barrera. (11-19-15). "More Mexicans leaving than coming to the U.S." Pew Research Center. Retrieved 2-20-17 from http://www.pewhispanic.org/2015/11/19/more-mexicans-leaving-than-coming-to-the-u-s/

[17] Ashifa Kassam and Jamiles Lartey. (1-30-17). Québec City mosque shooting: six dead as Trudeau condemns 'terrorist attack'. The Guardian, U.S. Edition. Retrieved 2-19-17 from https://www.theguardian.com/world/2017/jan/30/quebec-mosque-shooting-canada-deaths

[18] Jeremy Pressman and Erica Chenoweth. Crowd Estimates, 1.21.2017. Retrieved 2-19-17 from https://docs.google.com/spreadsheets/d/1xaoiLqYKz8x9Yc_rfhtmSOJQ2EGgeUVjvV4A8LsIaxY/edit#gid=0

[19] Reuters and Rebecca Harrington. (1-29-2017). Tens of thousands protest Trump's immigration ban in cities and airports across the US. Business Insider. Retrieved 2-19-17 from http://www.businessinsider.com/protest-photos-trump-muslim-immigration-ban-nyc-boston-dc-la-2017-1

[20] William C. Canby; Richard R. Clifton; and Michelle T. Friedland (2-9-2017). State of Washington, State of Minnesota v. Donald J. Trump, President of the United States, et. al. United States Court of Appeals for the Ninth Circuit. Retrieved 2-19-17 from http://cdn.ca9.uscourts.gov/datastore/opinions/2017/02/09/17-35105.pdf

[21] Joel Achenbach et. al. (7-8-16). "Five Dallas police officers were killed by a lone attacker, authorities say." The Washington Post. Retrieved 2-20-17 from https://www.washingtonpost.com/news/morning-mix/wp/2016/07/08/like-a-little-war-snipers-shoot-11-police-officers-during-dallas-protest-march-killing-five/?utm_term=.055ec46a605b

[22] Dylann Roof. lastrhodesian.com. Retrieved 2-12-17 from https://assets.documentcloud.org/documents/2108059/lastrhodesian-manifesto.pdf.

[23] Ibid.

[24] National Park Service. John Chivington biography. Sand Creek massacre. Retrieved 2-20-27 from https://www.nps.gov/sand/learn/historyculture/john-chivington-biography.htm

[25] Ibid.

[26] OKC bombing trial transcript. Oklahoman. Retrieved 5-27-2017 from http://newsok.com/article/1074993

[27] Brian Morton. (4-16-2009). The guns of spring. The Smirking Chimp. Retrieved 5-27-2017 from http://smirkingchimp.com/thread/21314

[28] Abraham Lincoln. (12-22-60). "To Alexander H. Stephens." Collected works of Abraham Lincoln, Vol. 4. Retrieved 2-20-17 from http://quod.lib.umich.edu/l/lincoln/lincoln4/1:250.1?rgn=div2;view=fulltext

[29] Wiley Sword. (4-1-2007). "Secession rather than dishonor" Pg. 25. Southern Invincibility. New York: St. Martin's Press.

[30] "Civil War Casualties." (2014). Civil War Trust. Retrieved 2-20-17 from http://www.civilwar.org/education/civil-war-casualties.html?referrer=https://www.google.com/

[31] This Day in History. John Wilkes Booth shoots Abraham Lincoln. The History Channel. Retrieved 2-20-17 from http://www.history.com/this-day-in-history/john-wilkes-booth-shoots-abraham-lincoln

[32] Biography.com Editors. (7-7-14). "Byron De La Beckwith Biography." A&E Television Networks. Retrieved 2-20-17 from http://www.biography.com/people/byron-de-la-beckwith-21442573

[33] Jessica Moore. (4-18-2002). The Medgar Evers Assassination. PBS Newshour. Retrieved 5-14-2017 from http://www.pbs.org/newshour/updates/media-jan-june02-evers_04-18/

[34] Samuel Momodu. (2007). The Birmingham Campaign (1963). BlackPast.org. Retrieved 5-14-2017 from http://www.blackpast.org/aah/birmingham-campaign-1963

[35] Nobelprize.com. Martin Luther King, Jr.: For civil rights and social justice. Retrieved 5-14-2017 from https://www.nobelprize.org/nobel_prizes/peace/laureates/1964/king-facts.html

[36] History.com staff. (2010). Selma to Montgomery march. History. Retrieved 5-14-2017 from http://www.history.com/topics/black-history/selma-montgomery-march

[37] Kevin J. Coleman. (7-20-2015). The Voting Rights Act of 1965: Background and overview. Congressional Research Service. Retrieved 5-14-2017 from https://fas.org/sgp/crs/misc/R43626.pdf

[38] Mark Berman. (2-10-2015). Even more black people were lynched in the U.S. than previously thought, study finds. Washington Post. Retrieved 5-14-2017 from https://www.washingtonpost.com/news/post-nation/wp/2015/02/10/even-more-black-people-were-lynched-in-the-u-s-than-previously-thought-study-finds/?utm_term=.eddcaa376570

[39] Robert A. Gibson. (1979). The Negro holocaust: Lynching and race riots in the United States, 1880-1950. Yale-New Haven Teachers Institute. Retrieved 5-14-2017 from http://teachersinstitute.yale.edu/curriculum/units/1979/2/79.02.04.x.html

[40] UPI. (9-17-1985). Death list names given to U.S. jury. New York Times. Retrieved 5-14-2017 from http://www.nytimes.com/1985/09/17/us/death-list-names-given-to-us-jury.html

[41] Nick Johansen. Alan Berg biography. IMDb. Retrieved 5-14-2017 from http://www.imdb.com/name/nm0073686/bio

[42] United States Constitution. (Ratified 1788). Retrieved 2-20-2017 from https://www.archives.gov/founding-docs/constitution-transcript

[43] Ibid.

[44] Mark D. Hall. (6-7-11). "Did America have a Christian founding?" The Heritage Foundation. Retrieved 2-20-17 from http://www.heritage.org/political-process/report/did-america-have-christian-founding

[45] Mark Edwards. (7-4-15). "Was America founded as a Christian nation?" CNN. Retrieved 2-20-17 from http://www.cnn.com/2015/07/02/living/america-christian-nation/

[46] Anti-abortion violence. Wikipedia.org. Retrieved 2-20-17 from https://en.wikipedia.org/wiki/Anti-abortion_violence

[47] National Abortion Federation. (2014). NAF violence and disruption statistics. Retrieved 6-25-2017 from http://5aa1b2xfmfh2e2mk03kk8rsx.wpengine.netdna-cdn.com/wp-content/uploads/Stats_Table_2014.pdf

[48] Anti-abortion violence. Wikipedia.

[49] Carrie Johnson. (6-27-16). "Supreme Court rules domestic abusers can lose their gun-ownership rights." National Public Radio. Retrieved 2-20-17 from http://www.npr.org/sections/thetwo-way/2016/06/27/483714423/supreme-court-rules-domestic-abusers-can-lose-their-gun-ownership-rights

Chapter 5

Howard Blum. (April, 2017). How ex-spy Christopher Steele compiled his explosive Trump-Russia dossier. Vanity Fair. Retrieved 4-30-2017 from http://www.vanityfair.com/news/2017/03/how-the-explosive-russian-dossier-was-compiled-christopher-steele

[2] Jordan Steffen. (12-9-2015). The Denver Post. Retrieved 7-1-2017 from http://www.denverpost.com/2015/12/09/planned-parenthood-suspect-i-am-guilty-a-warrior-for-the-babies/

[3] Michael Scherer. (9-30-2015). Fetus video referenced by Carly Fiorina released in full. TIME. Retrieved 6-26-2017 from http://time.com/4053578/abortion-carly-fiorina-planned-parenthood/

[4] Sam Reisman. (2-1-2016). Trump Tells Crowd to 'Knock the Crap Out' of Protesters, Offers to Pay Legal Fees. Mediaite. Retrieved 4-30-2017 from http://www.mediaite.com/online/trump-tells-crowd-to-knock-the-crap-out-of-protesters-offers-to-pay-legal-fees/

[5] Katayoun Kishi. (11-21-2016). Anti-Muslim assaults reach 9/11-era levels, FBI data show. Pew Research Center. Retrieved 4-30-2017 from http://www.pewresearch.org/fact-tank/2016/11/21/anti-muslim-assaults-reach-911-era-levels-fbi-data-show/

[6] Ibid.

[7] Rebecca Traister. (7-15-16). What mass killers really have in common. The Cut. New York Media, LLC. Retrieved 4-1-17 from http://nymag.com/thecut/2016/07/mass-killers-terrorism-domestic-violence.html

Chapter 6

Dave Umhoefer. (2-13-2013). Has Ryan remained consistent in talking about what he calls society's "takers" and "makers?" PolitiFact Wisconsin. Retrieved 5-25-2017 from http://www.politifact.com/wisconsin/statements/2013/feb/13/paul-ryan/has-ryan-remained-consistent-talking-about-what-h-/

[2] Molly Moorhead. (9-18-2012). Mitt Romney says 47 percent of Americans pay no income tax. PolitiFact. Retrieved 5-25-2017 from http://www.politifact.com/truth-o-meter/statements/2012/sep/18/mitt-romney/romney-says-47-percent-americans-pay-no-income-tax/

[3] NAFTA stands for North American Free Trade Agreement.

[4] Jon Greenberg. (9-29-2016). Was NAFTA 'worst trade deal ever'? Few agree. Retrieved 5-25-2017 from http://www.politifact.com/truth-o-meter/article/2016/sep/29/NAFTA-worst-trade-deal-ever-few-agree/

[5] Sara Chimene-Weiss, et al. Understanding the Iran-Contra affairs. Brown University. Retrieved 4-30-2017 from http://www.brown.edu/Research/Understanding_the_Iran_Contra_Affair/about.php

[6] Ibid.

[7] Ibid.

[8] George Tacopino and Chris Perez. (4-6-2017). US unleashes dozens of missiles on Syria in response to chemical attack. New York Post. Retrieved 4-30-2017 from http://nypost.com/2017/04/06/us-launches-airstrike-against-assad-after-syria-chemical-attack/

[9] Andrew Leonard. (6-4-2009). No, Jimmy Carter did it. Salon. Retrieved 4-30-2017 from http://www.salon.com/2009/06/04/jimmy_carter_did_it/

[10] Richard Tilly. (12-10-2009). Banking crises in three countries, 1890-1933: an historical and comparative perspective. Retrieved 5-26-2017 from https://www.ghi-dc.org/fileadmin/user_upload/GHI_Washington/PDFs/helmut_schmidt_prize_Richard_Tilly.pdf

[11] United States History. Great Depression Bank Crisis. Retrieved 5-26-2017 from http://www.u-s-history.com/pages/h1525.html

[12] Frontline. (5-8-2003). The long demise of Glass-Steagall. http://www.pbs.org/wgbh/pages/frontline/shows/wallstreet/weill/demise.html

[13] Kathleen A. Ruane. (7-13-2011). Fairness Doctrine: History and Constitutional issues. Congressional Research Service Report for Congress. Retrieved 5-25-2017 from https://fas.org/sgp/crs/misc/R40009.pdf

[14] United States Supreme Court. (6-9-1969). Red Lion Broadcasting Co., Inc. v. FCC. Retrieved 5-25-2017 from http://caselaw.findlaw.com/us-supreme-court/395/367.html

[15] Kathleen A. Ruane. Fairness Doctrine.

[16] New York Times. (9-23-1990). Confrontation in the gulf; Excerpts from Iraqi document on meeting with U.S. envoy. Retrieved 4-30-2017 from Internet Archive Wayback Machine at https://web.archive.org/web/20160324050102/http://www.nytimes.com/1990/09/23/world/confrontation-in-the-gulf-excerpts-from-iraqi-document-on-meeting-with-us-envoy.html?src=pm/&pagewanted=3

[17] Lauren Carroll. (5-10-2016). In context: Hillary Clinton's comments about coal jobs. PolitiFact. Retrieved 5-25-2017 from http://www.politifact.com/truth-o-meter/article/2016/may/10/context-hillary-clintons-comments-about-coal-jobs/

[18] Louis Jacobson. (8-9-2016). Donald Trump exaggerates Michigan job losses from coal regulations. PolitiFact. Retrieved 5-26-2017 from http://www.politifact.com/truth-o-meter/statements/2016/aug/09/donald-trump/donald-trump-exaggerates-michigan-job-losses-coal-

[19] U.S. Department of Energy. Wind vision: a new era for wind power in the United States. Page 34. Retrieved 5-26-2017 from https://www.energy.gov/sites/prod/files/wv_chapter2_wind_power_in_the_united_states.pdf

[20] Solar Energy Industries Association. Solar Industry Data. Retrieved 5-26-2017 from http://www.seia.org/research-resources/solar-industry-data

[21] Natural gas prices — historical chart. Interactive chart illustrating the history of Henry Hub natural gas prices. Macrotrends. Retrieved 5-26-2017 from http://www.macrotrends.net/2478/natural-gas-prices-historical-chart

[22] Robert Walton. (December 23, 2016). NRG completes conversion of 4 coal plants to burn natural gas. Utility Dive. Retrieved January 5, 2016 from http://www.utilitydive.com/news/nrg-completes-conversion-of-4-coal-plants-to-burn-natural-gas/433026/

[23] American Electric Power. Clinch River Plant receives new life as a natural gas plant. Retrieved 5-26-2017 from https://www.aep.com/environment/PlantRetirements/ClinchRiver.aspx

[24] Charlotte Cox, et al. (June 2015). Coal-to-gas switching. The American Oil & Gas Reporter. Retrieved 5-26-2017 from http://www.aogr.com/web-exclusives/exclusive-story/power-generators-turning-to-natural-gas

[25] CAFTA stands for Central American Free Trade Agreement; WTO is the World Trade Organization.

[26] Douglas A. Irwin. (July/August 2016). *The Truth About Trade*. Foreign Affairs. Retrieved January 4, 2017 from: https://www.foreignaffairs.com/articles/2016-06-13/truth-about-trade

[27] Trading Economics. United States employed persons. Retrieved 4-30-2017 from http://www.tradingeconomics.com/united-states/employed-persons

[28] David C. Johnston. (6-12-2015). The top .001 percent are different from you and me. Al Jazeera America. Retrieved 5-25-2017 from http://america.aljazeera.com/opinions/2015/6/the-top-001-percent-are-different-from-you-and-me.html

[29] Jason DeParle. (1-4-2012). Harder for Americans to rise from lower rungs. The New York Times. Retrieved 5-25-2017 from http://www.nytimes.com/2012/01/05/us/harder-for-americans-to-rise-from-lower-rungs.html?sq=mobility&st=cse&scp=1&pagewanted=all

Chapter 7

Ian Haney Lopez. (1-11-14). The racism at the heart of the Reagan presidency. Salon. Retrieved 3-30-17 from http://www.salon.com/2014/01/11/the_racism_at_the_heart_of_the_reagan_presidency/

[2] Ian Haney Lopez. (2-28-14). Six Case Studies in Dog Whistle Politics. Moyers & Company. Retrieved 3-30-17 from http://billmoyers.com/content/six-case-studies-in-dog-whistle-politics/3/

[3] Ian Haney Lopez. (1-14-14). Dog Whistle Politics: How Politicians Use Coded Racism to Push Through Policies Hurting All. Democracy Now. Retrieved 3-31-17 from https://www.democracynow.org/2014/1/14/dog_whistle_politics_how_politicians_use

[4] Rebecca Kaplan. (1-8-14). Lawmakers mark the 50th anniversary of LBJ's "war on poverty" speech. CBS News. Retrieved 3-31-17 from

http://www.cbsnews.com/news/lawmakers-mark-the-50th-anniversary-of-lbjs-war-on-poverty-speech/

[5] Anne Gearan, et al. (12-4-17). Trump's Taiwan phone call was long planned, say people who were involved. The Washington Post. Retrieved 4-1-17 from https://www.washingtonpost.com/politics/trumps-taiwan-phone-call-was-weeks-in-the-planning-say-people-who-were-involved/2016/12/04/f8be4b0c-ba4e-11e6-94ac-3d324840106c_story.html?utm_term=.8b79c2d91fc2

[6] the World Bank Group. (2017.) China: overview. Retrieved 5-20-2017 from http://www.worldbank.org/en/country/china/overview

[7] Eleanor Ross. (3-29-2017). How and why China is building islands in the South China Sea. Newsweek. Retrieved 5-20-2017 from http://www.newsweek.com/china-south-china-sea-islands-build-military-territory-expand-575161

[8] United States Constitution, Amendment XIV, Section 1. "All persons born or naturalized in the United States and subject to the jurisdiction thereof, are citizens of the United States..."

[9] Michelle Malkin. (11-13-2015). The myth of H-1B job creation. National Review. Retrieved 5-20-2017 from http://www.nationalreview.com/article/426989/myth-h-1b-job-creation-michelle-malkin

[10] PracticeLink. (Fall 2009). Physician Compensation Worldwide. Retrieved 4-30-2017 from https://journal.practicelink.com/vital-stats/physician-compensation-worldwide/

[11] Supreme Court of the United States. (1954). Transcript of Brown v. Board of Education. Retrieved 4-1-17 from https://ourdocuments.gov/doc.php?doc=87&page=transcript

[12] Library of Congress. (2004). Brown v. Board at Fifty: With an even hand. Retrieved 4-1-17 from https://www.loc.gov/exhibits/brown/brown-brown.html

[13] Bernadette D. Proctor, et al. (September, 2016). Income and poverty in the United States: 2015, Page 15. Current population reports — U.S. Census Bureau. Retrieved 4-1-17 from https://www.census.gov/content/dam/Census/library/publications/2016/demo/p60-256.pdf

[14] Noreen C. McDonald, et al. (2014). Costs of school transportation: quantifying the fiscal impacts of encouraging walking and bicycling for school travel. Springer Science+Business Media. New York. http://mcdonald.web.unc.edu/files/2014/12/McDonaldetal_CostsSchoolTrans.pdf

[15] Marin R. West. (10-23-2014). Why do Americans rate their local public schools so favorably? Brookings. Retrieved 5-1-2017 from https://www.brookings.edu/research/why-do-americans-rate-their-local-public-schools-so-favorably

Chapter 8
HMS Gurkha (F20). Wikipedia. Retrieved 5-20-2017 from https://en.wikipedia.org/wiki/HMS_Gurkha_(F20)

Chapter 10
Paul Krugman. Weakened at Bernie's. New York Times - Blog. Retrieved 5-20-2017 from https://krugman.blogs.nytimes.com/2016/01/19/weakened-at-bernies/?_r=0

[2] Bernie Sanders. (2016). Medicare for all. Retrieved 6-30-2017 from https://berniesanders.com/issues/medicare-for-all/

[3] CMS.gov. (1-20-2016). Retrieved 6-30-2017 from https://www.cms.gov/

Research-Statistics-Data-and-Systems/Statistics-Trends-and-Reports/NationalHealthExpendData/NationalHealthAccountsHistorical.html
4 CMS.gov. (6-14-2017). Retrieved 6-30-2017 from https://www.cms.gov/Research-Statistics-Data-and-Systems/Statistics-Trends-and-Reports/NationalHealthExpendData/NHE-Fact-Sheet.html
5 Sabrina Ali. (5-10-2016). What are the profit margins in the healthcare industry? Retrieved 6-30-2017 from https://www.quora.com/What-are-the-profit-margins-in-the-healthcare-industry
6 The Henry J. Kaiser Family Foundation. (9-29-2016). Retrieved 6-30-2017 from http://www.kff.org/uninsured/fact-sheet/key-facts-about-the-uninsured-population/

Chapter 12
Rachel Cao. (11-9-2017). Canadian immigration website crashes on election night. CNBC. Retrieved 5-20-2017 from http://www.cnbc.com/2016/11/09/canadian-immigration-website-crashes-on-election-night.html
2 Sebastian Brandt. (1622). A Jamestown settler describes life in Virginia, 1622. Retrieved January 7, 2016 from https://www.gilderlehrman.org/history-by-era/early-settlements/resources/jamestown-settler-describes-life-virginia-1622
3 Joseph Stromberg. (April 13, 2013). Starving Settlers in Jamestown Colony Resorted to Cannibalism. Smithsonian. Retrieved January 7, 2016 from http://www.smithsonianmag.com/history/starving-settlers-in-jamestown-colony-resorted-to-cannibalism-46000815/
4 Scott Horsley. (1-29-2017). Ahead of Trump's first jobs report a look at his remarks on the numbers. NPR. Retrieved 7-6-2017 from http://www.npr.org/2017/01/29/511493685/ahead-of-trumps-first-jobs-report-a-look-at-his-remarks-on-the-numbers
5 Jana Heigl. (3-21-2017). A timeline of Trump's false wiretapping charge. PolitiFact. Retrieved 7-6-2017 from http://www.politifact.com/truth-o-meter/article/2017/mar/21/timeline-donald-trumps-false-wiretapping-charge/
6 Lindsay Dodgson. (11-11-2016). The biggest threat to Earth has been dismissed by Trump as a Chinese hoax. Retrieved 5-20-2017 from http://www.businessinsider.com/donald-trump-climate-change-chinese-hoax-2016-11
7 Jeremy Diamond. (2-7-2017). Trump falsely claims US murder rate is 'highest' in 47 years. CNN. Retrieved 5-20-2017 from http://www.cnn.com/2017/02/07/politics/donald-trump-murder-rate-fact-check/
8 Rafael Bernal. (3-19-2017). Reports find that immigrants commit less crime than US-born citizens. The Hill. Retrieved 5-20-2017 from http://thehill.com/latino/324607-reports-find-that-immigrants-commit-less-crime-than-us-born-citizens
9 Lindsay Dodgson. (11-9-2016). US president-elect Donald Trump has said vaccines cause autism, and he couldn't be more wrong. Retrieved 5-20-2017 from http://www.businessinsider.com/trump-vaccines-autism-2016-11
10 Kurt Eichenwald. (9-29-16). How Donald Trump's company violated the United States embargo against Cuba. Newsweek. Retrieved 5-20-2017 from http://www.newsweek.com/2016/10/14/donald-trump-cuban-embargo-castro-violated-florida-504059.html

[11] David A. Fahrenthold. (9-20-2016). Trump used $258,000 from his charity to settle legal problems. The Washington Post. Retrieved 5-20-2017 from https://www.washingtonpost.com/politics/trump-used-258000-from-his-charity-to-settle-legal-problems/2016/09/20/adc88f9c-7d11-11e6-ac8e-cf8e0dd91dc7_story.html?utm_term=.c1d9ab90069d
[12] Donald Trump. (10-24-2016). St. Augustine, FL. YouTube. Retrieved 6-27-2017 from https://www.youtube.com/watch?v=bcCxGZ-y48w

Chapter 14

Legal Information Institute. Standard Oil Co. of New Jersey v. United States. Cornell University Law School. Retrieved 5-21-2017 from https://www.law.cornell.edu/supremecourt/text/221/1#writing-USSC_CR_0221_0001_ZX

[2] Ida M. Tarbell. (1904). The history of the Standard Oil Company. Pages 56-69. Retrieved 5-21-2017 from https://openlibrary. org/books/OL7057056M/The_history_of_the_Standard_Oil_Company

[3] Frontline. (5-8-2003). The long demise of Glass-Steagall. http://www.pbs.org/wgbh/pages/frontline/shows/wallstreet/weill/demise.html

[4] National Labor Relations Board. The 1935 passage of the Wagner Act. Retrieved 6-13-2017 from https://www.nlrb.gov/who-we-are/our-history/1935-passage-wagner-act

[5] Charles Donahue. The Davis-Bacon Act and the Walsh-Healey Public Contracts Act: a comparison of coverage and minimum wage provisions. Duke University Law. Retrieved 6-13-2017 from http://scholarship.law.duke.edu/cgi/viewcontent.cgi?article=3009&context=lcp

[6] J. Fair Grossman. Labor Standards Act of 1938: Maximum struggle for a minimum wage. U.S. Department of Labor. Retrieved 6-131-2017 from https://www.dol.gov/oasam/programs/history/flsa1938.htm

Acknowledgements

Many thanks to Jackson Harper, Marcia Kahn, and Melanie Zhou for reading early drafts and offering thoughtful and much-needed criticism. Special thanks to Ric Rawlins for helping me form a coherent response to conspiracy theorists. Thanks to Tasha Brown for being an awesome sounding board. Thanks also to Guttorm Fjeldstad and Anders Utgaard for providing online access to their detailed account of the restoration of Ju88 U4+TK. Finally, I am forever grateful to Amy Love, my wife, who read the earliest drafts and encouraged me to continue, and who is always supportive of my writing endeavors.

❧❧

Voting Information

If you are not registered to vote, or if you have moved since the last time you voted, changed your name, or you just are not sure, go to this non-partisan website, courtesy of the federal government, to find out how to register and vote in your area: **https://vote.gov/**
This is a very simple process. In most states it takes only three to four minutes to complete a voter registration form. As of the publication date of Speaker for the Powerless, 31 states have on-line registration. And most important of all, your country is depending upon your well-informed participation.

About the Author

Todd Lederman teaches at a Jefferson County, Colorado elementary charter school for which he also serves on the Board of Directors. He has written several children's stories and a children's novel, *Notch Ear's Sacrifice*, as well as short fiction for adults and political essays dating back to the 1980's. Prior to his nearly two-decade long second career in education, he developed and managed hotels, resort area condominiums, apartments and a bank.

Order copies of Speaker for the Powerless at the author's website: **https://sites.google.com/site/toddledermanauthor/** Or visit the website and take a tour of other titles.

www.ingramcontent.com/pod-product-compliance
Lightning Source LLC
Chambersburg PA
CBHW031547260326
41914CB00002B/308